Pride amid Prejudice

A Soldier's Memoir

Pride amid Prejudice
A Soldier's Memoir

Chief Warrant Officer (Ret'd)
Necole E. Belanger, MMM, CD, BMASc

DOUBLE‡DAGGER

PRAISE FOR PRIDE AMID PREJUDICE

The professional relationship between service members, regardless of rank, service, or occupation, is fundamental to success on the battlefield. A strong relationship built on mutual trust and respect sets the working conditions that leads to folks going that extra mile in challenging and oftentimes hazardous situations. Regrettably, this isn't the case when that relationship is made fragile or weak because of personal bias, fear, or intimidation. It takes a strong and determined individual to work through the latter and to put the needs of the unit ahead of theirs; this is what CWO Necole Belanger has done throughout her military career, and the results are not surprising — on the one hand success in the workplace, and on the other hand a personal toll on her authentic self. I have had the pleasure to know and work with Necole in the latter stages of my own military career, and the fact that I wasn't aware of the inner struggles she recounts in her book speaks to her strong sense of commitment, dedication, and integrity, and to her unwavering sense of personal pride and desire to do well for herself and those around her. Necole's words may make you question the Canadian Armed Forces as an institution and will make you wonder if culture change will ever come. You will also come away with a strong sense of personal triumph and desire to see change happen. Necole, you inspire me in so many ways — thank you for opening up your heart for others to better understand.

- **Christine Whitecross, LGen (Ret'd)**

Necole's memoire is a cautionary tale that needs to be read by all humanity; the lovers, the haters, and everyone in between. At one level it is the story of how the Canadian Armed Forces failed in its covenant to ensure her wellbeing while she so faithfully and diligently served Canada. At another level it is about the cost of being marginalized, abused, and discounted over a thirty-five-year career and the very real harm, physical, mental, and emotional, that results. But at its core, it is an excruciatingly human story about passion and perseverance through adversity, a struggle for personal growth, a pursuit of professional excellence, and a final redemption and freedom. You won't make it through without laughing and crying as Necole calls it the way she sees it with her blunt perspective, wry sense of humour, and her principled character and judgment. While the CAF has made some progress, it still has a long way to go in ensuring an inclusive environment for all its dedicated professionals — they deserve nothing less, and certainly Necole deserved better.

- W.G. Cummings, LCol (Ret'd)

Raw and emotional. An enlightening and very personal story; this book is provocative yet necessary. Necole narrates from a place of self-revelation and self-healing. I could not be prouder of her for having the courage to open up and share her journey with us. My own military story is so like Necole's, and I must admit that although I found it very difficult to read at times (due to the unrealized and pent-up emotions of my own survival story from the LGBT Purge), I also couldn't put it down.

This book has accelerated my own path to understanding and healing, and I suspect that there are thousands of others who can empathize through their own lived experiences, but thousands more who had no idea that the LGBT Purge even happened. I'm so proud of Necole for sharing her story and shining her light on the often-unfair landscape of gender and diversity. There are so many of us who have trudged similar paths and triumphed despite this, but so many more who broke down. I hope this book helps them too.

- Colleen Halpin, Maj (Ret'd)

Copyright 2023 Necole Belanger

All rights reserved. No part of this publication may be reproduced or transmitted in any form or by any means, electronically or mechanically including photocopying, recording or any information storage or retrieval system, without prior permission in writing from the author.

*Library and Archives Canada Cataloguing in Publication
Belanger, Necole, author
Pride amid Prejudice / Necole Belanger*

Issued in print and electronic formats.

ISBN: 978-1-990644-83-2 (soft cover)
ISBN: 978-1-990644-85-6 (hardcover)
ISBN: 978-1-990644-84-9 (e-pub)

*Editor: Rachel Spence
Cover design: Pablo Javier Herrera
Interior design: Winston A. Prescott*

Double Dagger Books Ltd
*Toronto, Ontario, Canada
www.doubledagger.ca*

Table of Contents

Introduction 1
1. I Always Knew 3
2. Human Cruelty Knows No Limits 13
3. Recruit Course 8746 — Ready Aye Ready 21
4. The Impact of Trauma 39
5. Locked in My Cage with Guilt and Shame 43
6. The Purge 47
7. Come Out Come Out, Whoever You Are 53
8. My Eventual Saviour 65
9. Deployments—Jakarta, Bosnia, Cyprus, and the Return Home 70
10. Loudership versus Leadership 87
11. The Lonely Walk to the Fifth Floor 97
12. Tactician versus Strategist 109
13. The Big Leagues — I Had Finally Arrived, or Had I? 116
14. If It Was So Bad, Why Stay Thirty-Five Years? 124
15. Trusted to Serve 127
16. My Final Farewell 132
Epilogue 137
Acknowledgements 140
Additional Reading 143

Introduction

BESIDES THE OBVIOUS, that I am a married lesbian who achieved the rank of Chief Warrant Officer and finished my career as the Command Chief Warrant Officer for the Canadian Forces Intelligence Command, what else do you know about me? I think this exposé of my life will shock even those closest to me because I created a persona that was of this no-nonsense Justice League–type of female fighter for transparency and fairness. In general, my public life was usually one that was "put together," maybe even normal or perfect. This was so far from the truth, especially during my last couple of years of service. During a time and in a position where my voice should have had the most influence, it had none. The higher I went in rank, the more insignificant I became. I denied this right up until the very end, and I pretended to be fine — to my own demise.

During my final years of service, I challenged, to the best of my ability, the oftentimes nepotistic culture that existed just under the surface of the Canadian Armed Forces Non-Commissioned Member succession planning process in order to keep the process fair and just. It was exhausting and terribly demoralizing knowing that my voice carried no weight unless it was supported by one of my male counterparts. I did what I had to do, at the time, to survive and to make the little changes the system allowed me to. Additionally, I was able to effect change through some major institutional projects if I allowed others to lay claim to my work.

The cost of having to do business this way was extremely high, and I suffered from "smiling depression" — when someone appears happy and carefree on the outside but is actually unhappy and depressed underneath their "smiling" facade. Those who know me, including my loved ones, had no idea I was experiencing depression because I appeared to be in full control. I was cheerful, optimistic, and happy. I had learned to put on a false smile since childhood and I became an expert at pretending that nothing bothered me. Then again, as you make your way through the chapters of this book, you will come to learn that my perceived happiness was all a facade. I believed that showing signs of depression was a weakness, and because others had it worse, that I shouldn't complain.

I battled my own demons for most of my life but never shared the burden with anyone. That was until it all came tumbling down. I felt like Humpty Dumpty, and no matter how much I drank to forget, denied that I was held to a different standard, that I was not part of the inner circle, or pretended to be someone I wasn't, all my mentees and loved ones were unable to put me back together again.

In writing this book, I finally found the courage to be honest with myself and others, and I've started to pick up the pieces of my inner self.

1
I Always Knew

Being homosexual is no more abnormal than being lefthanded.
— *Abhijit Naskar*

IT WAS A COLD AND GREY MORNING in early December 1963 when my mother went into labour. My father, a sailor in Canada's Royal Canadian Navy (RCN), made plans with the neighbour to take care of my sister and brother, who were three and two years old, respectively. He called a taxi to take my mom to the hospital. Unfortunately, I could not have picked a worse time to want to enter this world. The early morning traffic on the Sir John A. MacDonald Bridge was bumper to bumper. Luckily, the Military Police (MP) had been parked near the toll booth and took notice of a panicked young sailor getting out of a taxi to retrieve the dime he had tossed at the toll basket and missed, on three separate attempts, while his very pregnant wife screamed at him, "Hurry up, Guy, this one isn't going to wait." Although comical to watch the struggle of this soon-to-be new dad, the MP intervened and provided an escort across the bridge, complete with lights and siren. I do not know if it was the police escort or not, but I came out of the womb knowing I wanted to be a police officer. Two other things also became crystal clear by the time I was five years old: I was lefthanded and I was gay, even though I did not yet know what that meant.

Not once since I decided that I was going to be a cop did I waiver in this conviction. A lot of this steadfastness had to do with my television idol, Angie Dickinson, who was the lead actress in the weekly series, Police Woman. I wanted to be just like her, although three-and-a-half years of waiting until the MP occupation opened back up for recruitment in 1987 did try that patience at times. I wanted to live a career within my calling, to defend my country, uphold its ideals, regulations, and principles. Only they didn't want me. Homosexuals, according to the Government of Canada, were an aberration, and more importantly, they were a threat to Canada's national security. The country that I was ready to lay my life down for didn't want me because I could not be trusted, simply because of who I loved.

From a young age, I constantly tried to reject the fact that I was gay, even well into my adulthood. I tried to deny my authentic self because society believed it to be a sin. My own family believed it was a sin.

Like any military family, our father was always away at sea or on deployments to a foreign land, which to us could have been the moon for all we knew. Our mother, the backbone of our family, taught us three basic moral principles: don't lie, don't cheat, and don't steal. She was the chief disciplinarian in the family and fulfilled every other role a child needed from a parent. My mom may not have worn one of the Canadian Armed Forces (CAF) uniforms, but she shared the burden of service. Sometimes, as you can imagine with three children all under the age of five, we could be a handful and our transgressions were plentiful. Just as one of us would exit our terrible twos, another one would enter. My mother's favourite saying in those early years was "wait till your father gets home." Fortunately for us, that could be anywhere from a day to six months, so the threat quickly lost its potency the older we got. My mom would often forget our transgressions by the time my dad got back from sea.

I spent my first twelve years growing up at Canadian Forces Base (CFB) Shearwater. I have such fond memories of those times, starting from grade 1 when I experienced my first crush — on my teacher, Ms. MacDonald. She always made me feel so special, letting me empty the garbage cans and clean the chalkboards after school. She sensed that I was different from the other children, but she was always there to protect me if the kids in my class were picking on me for being the teacher's pet. All I knew was that I did not want to graduate into grade 2 because that would mean I would no longer have Ms. MacDonald for a homeroom teacher. I did graduate and move into grade 2 and I soon forgot all about Ms. MacDonald, but I did not forget how certain girls made me feel inside.

When I got a little older, once or twice a week after supper I used to take my little red plastic ball glove, get on my bike, and head on over to the baseball diamond, across from the gymnasium, to watch the military women play softball, hoping they would let me play with them. Even though I was only ten years old at the time, I felt a kinship to these ladies. To this day, I can still recall how happy I was when one lady would take notice of me standing along the third base line and come and toss the ball with me during innings. Interestingly enough, I met this lady about a decade later, and about 2,500 kilometres away, in Trenton. She was still in the military and still playing ball. As for me, instead of watching from the third base line, I was playing third base for a local civilian team. Instead of a little red plastic glove, I had graduated to an adult size brown leather glove. She never put two and two together and I never told her, even after having a one-night stand with her.

Although I could not understand this sense of belonging, I knew I was different. Society strongly transmitted and enforced heterosexual behaviour back then, and most people received the message loud and clear. As such, they would act in accordance with society's definition of their gender. Somehow, that message did not decode itself in my brain. I felt isolated, alone, and very afraid. My father was quick to recognize that society's message got scrambled in my head because he told my mother that he thought I was gay. I would hear them whispering to themselves after they thought I was asleep. According to my father, I displayed all the stereotypical signs of a lesbian: I excelled at sports, preferred trucks and toy guns over strollers and dolls, I hated wearing dresses, and I always had to have my hair cut short. Then there was the time when I was around five or six years old when I told all the little girls in the neighbourhood that I was a boy so they would kiss me. This worked for a while until one of them caught me peeing in the woods and asked my mother, "If Nicki is a boy, why does he squat to pee like I do?" The jig was up and that was the last time I kissed a girl until I was seventeen years old.

I was so mad at myself that day for getting caught peeing in the woods by that little girl, not only because the girls would not kiss me anymore but because they all knew my dirty little secret and the teasing began. Shame is a very powerful emotion that shaped my life, both from a personal and professional standpoint. Experiencing shame made me feel worthless, embarrassed, and humiliated of who I was. If others were to find out and learn my dirty little secret, I would be teased or judged in a negative manner, like when one little girl's mother forbade her child from playing with me. Maybe she thought her daughter might "catch the gay," like you would catch the common cold! Instead of being mad at the mother, I felt sorry for her child, because the pain on that little girl's face seemed worse than mine. I realized that day that every family has secrets and nobody can know what goes on behind closed doors.

I was twelve years old when we moved from Shearwater to CFB Trenton. I had become particularly good at keeping my shame hidden away, but unfortunately it thrived on burying itself in the deep, dark crevices of my mind. My mom was ecstatic about the move because she was coming home. Both her and my dad grew up in Marmora, Ontario, approximately thirty minutes from Trenton. My sister was devastated, as was my brother, who were both in high school and leaving behind boyfriends and girlfriends. I was entering grade eight and I personally could not have cared one way or the other. By then I was already miserable. I had no friends, nor did I want any — I did not want a friend to see what I had to watch.

For years, every weekend my father would come home drunk, pick fights with my mother, then physically and emotionally abuse my sister and brother. For the most part, I learned to stay out of his way when he was drinking, and if I could not avoid him, I would do everything I could think of to suck up to him. I became so good at it that my siblings referred to me as "Daddy's little suck up." It obviously worked as I very rarely got a beating or was grounded. However, kowtowing to him left me feeling sick to my stomach, even at that age. To this day, my siblings have no idea just how much I despised this man, who was supposed to be our dad. His role was to provide love and support that would help the three of us flourish as we were growing. He failed in his role; he was supposed to love his children, not hurt them. I could not understand how he could be proud of me one minute and within an hour the same day be hurting me with whatever weapon he had in his hands.

His behaviour ultimately prepared me well for coping in a male-dominated military. Whether I wanted to admit it or not, my father set me up for success in the military by providing me with a macho, hypermasculine role model to follow and emulate. Through his example I avoided or diminished most trauma visited upon me or perpetrated against me, and I quickly learned to not trust anyone, especially those close to me.

The feelings of inadequacy, brought on by one very cruel parent, made me struggle to cope with my sexuality. I hated who I was. I was a freak of nature, or at least that is what I thought at that age. Each night, in the darkness of my bedroom, I would ask myself why God could not have made me normal, like my brother and sister. Why did God make me this way? Even then I struggled with looking for answers as to why I was attracted to girls, but none came. As hard as I clasped my little hands together to pray, he never answered my prayers.

Constantly looking over my shoulder, leading a double life from friends and family, and masquerading as a straight person was exhausting. I was so paranoid about being found out that I would pretend to be homophobic to throw people off my trail. I did this for a very long time, not accepting my same sex attractions. I internalized homophobia and I felt the need to pick on openly gay people, not because I hated them but because I was jealous of their will to be themselves. I, on the other hand, was deeply in the closet. I even had a boyfriend all through high school! Brian was an amazing guy, but I came to realize that I was fooling myself and him and it was not fair to either of us. We broke up in grade 12.

For anyone who thinks that being gay is a choice, you are wrong! Let me ask you this: Did you choose to be straight, or did it just happen naturally? So, if it just happened automatically for you, in that your brain was hardwired to think that way, what makes you think the process was any different for me? Now ask yourself this, because trust me, I have asked myself these very same questions more than once in my life: Why would someone choose this life, why would someone choose to live a lie, to hide their authentic self, to be made fun of or beat up or even kicked out of the family home simply because of who they loved? Nobody in their right mind would choose that! Just like I had no choice being a lefty. Being left-handed in the 1960s and 1970s was thought to be a symptom of mental and moral deficiency. Often the pencil would be taken out of my left hand and placed in my right. The result: I am now ambidextrous.

Being a left-handed lesbian, I wanted to make up for what society deemed my internal shortcomings. I wanted to be an all-star athlete. I would often ask my brother to help me get better at sports. To improve my baseball skills, especially my catching skills, he decided to tie me to the fence and throw baseballs at me as hard as he could. I had no choice but to catch them or get seriously injured.

He also trained me in other sports as well. Badminton, squash, and hockey were some of our favourites to play. After about two years in Trenton, I started to play organized hockey and developed a secret crush on one of the girls on my team. I figured this was a safe attraction because I had been dating Brian since the beginning of grade 8, and because I had a boyfriend, she would not think to question my sexuality, or at least that was what I thought. We spent time together on weekends and were good friends. Thank God I never said anything to her about my feelings because one day when I came into the dressing room, I overheard her and two other girls making fun of me. One of the girls was saying that she thought I was creepy and that I stared at everyone while they were getting changed. Naturally, they stopped when they saw me and I pretended that I did not hear them, but my heart shattered into a million pieces that day. Is that what all straight girls thought — that just because I was gay that it meant that I would stare at all girls? Their comments reinforced the shame and humiliation I felt. I was so hurt, and I felt truly betrayed by my friend. I could not fathom why someone would think I would stare at them. In fact, I took extra care to never look up in the dressing room because I did not want anyone to accuse of me of that very thing. It was the first of many times in my life where I would experience such outward distain directed at me.

After being exposed to such bigotry, I emotionally detached, and at the age of fourteen, I started to abuse alcohol, which I would steal from my parents' liquor cabinet. I used the alcohol to numb myself to the point where I isolated myself from others who were not my immediate family. I drank to lower my inhibitions. I drank to forget. I could not talk to anyone — nobody knew what I was feeling inside because nobody knew for sure that I was gay, which made for an extremely lonely childhood. Drinking made me feel happy and more confident; when drunk I felt a reprieve from the shame-game I was playing with myself while I was sober. My drive to be "normal" was making me weak. As much as I despised my father for drinking too much and being cruel and oblivious to other people's feelings, I was becoming just like him. I would do things when drunk that I would never consider doing when I was sober. I would sleep with strange men, trying to prove to myself that I was not gay, trying to convince myself that they just were not the right one for me. The truth was none of them were Mr. Right because I was secretly coveting Ms. Right.

During this time in my life, I would even engage in behaviours that would endanger my life. When I was sixteen years old, I dove off a thirty-foot pier into three feet of water. Of course, one must ask why. I was not consciously trying to end my life, but as I think back, I just did not seem to care anymore about self-preservation. I wanted to celebrate my big swimming gold medal win in the 400-

and 800-metre freestyle and the 200-metre individual medley at the provincial championships the weekend prior, so I called in sick to work and went out drinking with my friends instead. Like my sister and brother before me, I worked at Wong's Chinese Food Restaurant washing dishes. My friends and I decided to go to the Trenton pier. Some people were on the dam side of the pier, jumping off the bridge into the water below, while others, myself included, were on the calm side of the locks. Alice came to get me to jump with her on the dam side. Showing off, I decided to dive off the pier. I hit bottom! I sprung up out of the water and was immediately blinded by the blood gushing from my head, nose, and mouth. Alice and a few others jumped in and carried me out of the water. It was a good thing I did not lose consciousness because the undertow would have drowned me. My friends put me in the car and drove me to the hospital where the doctor stitched me up and then walked me through the paraplegic ward. Before letting me leave the hospital, he looked at me and said, "You better change your ways, little miss, or you are going to find yourself in here, or worse!"

By the time I was released from the hospital and got dropped off at home, my parents were asleep, thank God. I quietly went to bed, still covered in my own blood. The next morning when I got up, I had a goose egg on my forehead so large that when I bent forward, I fell over. My eyes had swollen shut but did not turn black. I had stitches in my forehead, stitches in my lip and stitches keeping my nose together. I was quite the sight. I was unrecognizable. I walked out into the kitchen and my poor mother almost had a heart attack.

"What in the hell happened to you? Did someone beat you up?"

"Not exactly," I replied sheepishly, explaining what happened.

"Oh my God, Necole, you could have been killed. Has your father seen you yet?"

"Not yet."

"Come with me. We need to get that dried blood out of your hair."

My mom was great like that. Often, and whenever she could, she would hide our wrongdoings from our father so we did not have to incur his wrath. Unfortunately, she was not going to be able to hide this transgression from him. I obediently followed my mother down into the basement to the laundry sink, where she not-so-gently washed the blood out of my hair. With my head under the sink and the water running, I heard my mom mutter to herself, "I hope your dress fits Holly (my brother's wife) because there is no way you can be your sister's wedding looking like that." I was glad my head was under the tap because tears instantly sprang to my eyes, and I did not want her to see how her words had wounded me. It was the most important day of my sister's life and I was going to ruin it.

After getting cleaned up I met with my dad. He took one look at me, demanded to know what happened, and then proceeded to ground me for two weeks and forbade me from hanging out with Alice. I think he was madder that I lied, rather than afraid that I could have killed myself. My dad took away the little television he had given me as a reward for my swimming feats the week before, telling me I did not deserve it. Just one more thing I did to disappoint those I loved the most. And if that was not bad enough, when I was finally able to return to the pool, I was afraid to dive off the starting blocks. Even if I could start in the water, I could not do a flip turn because my depth perception was all screwed up from smacking my head so hard. Halfway through swim practice, I slammed my arm down on top of the water and, with tears in my eyes, exited the pool. I never swam again. The pool was the one place where I felt confident, where I did not feel like a freak. Now that was gone! I retreated into myself, creating a safe space so I could not be hurt anymore, by anyone, even those who were supposed to love me unconditionally. I stayed there for an exceptionally long time. In case you are wondering, I did end up being in my sister's wedding, but I never did get my little TV back — my dad sold it.

The rest of my high school years went by without incident. Then, in grade 12, I met a woman whose name was Annette. She was twelve years my senior and separated from her husband. We started a secret affair, my first lesbian experience. It felt so right. I wanted to spend all my time with her, so I moved out of my parents' house and into my twenty-nine-year-old girlfriend's house. I was seventeen at the time. I finished out my high school year, but according to my father, I was breaking my mother's heart. He asked me to come back home to go to college, for my mother's sake. I would do anything for my mother, so that summer I moved home, and in September I started my first year of college. It only took two weeks into the summer before college for my relationship with Annette to start showing significant cracks. With such a vast age difference between us and the fact that she had a husband, our relationship ended. I tried to buckle down and put all my energy into my studies so that I could fulfill my dream of joining the CAF and becoming a MP, but something kept calling me back to the lesbian underworld — and then I met Tracy.

2
HUMAN CRUELTY KNOWS NO LIMITS

OURS WAS A TYPICAL MILITARY FAMILY upbringing: going to military schools, living in military housing, and having a parent who was never around. Ever since I was around twelve years of age, I remember my mom saying that my dad was a good provider but a shitty husband and father. My siblings and I agreed. On the odd occasion when he was around, it seemed as if he had time for all the other kids in the neighbourhood except his own. If the other kids in the neighbourhood asked him to jump in and play or push them or fix something, he always did it and enjoyed it. If we asked him to play with us, he was too busy, and as to fixing things for us, it was always on his time, not ours. But he was a good provider. He would take all his annual leave in the fall and go pick apples at an orchard and then give my mom all the money he earned so she could buy Christmas presents for us. We never went without when it came to material things.

Despite this one redeeming trait, my father was as cruel as they came. The actions of one very cruel parent made me struggle to cope with who I was. My dad always overreacted to situations. Once, my brother and I were playing street hockey in the driveway and my dad, who was in the kitchen with my mom doing dishes, told us not to play there because we were going to break a window. We ignored him, and guess what? We broke a window! He was outside screaming at us to get inside before I could even formulate the thought in my mind that we were in for one hell of a beating for that misdemeanor. My brother was in the door first and up the stairs before my father could get in a good position to smack him. I, however, was not that lucky. He had the cast iron frying pan in his hand. He hit me over the head with it. That rang my bell and made my knees go weak, but I would never give him the satisfaction of hearing me cry out in pain or seeing me go down out of weakness.

I did not know it at the time, but my father terrorized and bullied us because he had his own unresolved trauma with his father, who bullied and abused him. My dad left home at sixteen years old and joined the military just to escape the tyranny of his father. The psychological wounds and trauma that he suffered as a boy and that had accumulated inside him over decades were transferred onto us. Whenever we were in trouble, he would do what he knew — he would hit you with whatever was in his hands. His preferred weapon of choice was his belt, which ironically was the CAF standard issue black leather belt with simple brass buckle. (I guess you could say I was getting abused by the CAF long before I enrolled!)

After one of my brother's transgressions, my sister and I had the bright idea of telling our brother to put on as many long john pants as he could and then we shoved Sears catalogues down his pants. Once he had everything on and in place, we would pinch him to see if he could feel it. Honestly, there was no way he was going to feel the beating he was about to get, even if my dad used the buckle, as he had done before. With ten pairs of long john pants on he could barely walk. When it was his time to head downstairs to face my dad, my sister and I watched from the top of the stairs. She and I silently started laughing when the sweat was rolling off my brother's forehead because, this was the one time he did not get a beating. My dad decided to talk to him for almost thirty minutes. My poor brother must have sweat off twenty pounds in that time.

My sister had it the worst. I think my father deemed her the easiest prey between the three of us. She was grounded from the age of thirteen until she left home to get married. She and my father never agreed on anything, and putting the two of them in a room together was like trying to mix oil and water. I think by the time it got to me, he was just too tired most of the time because I was worse than the two of my siblings combined. I learned from them how to not get caught. I also learned to suck up to my dad, which my siblings refused to do. They had way more integrity than I did. No wonder my mom was always happy when my dad would go to sea. We would have peace and we could act like a normal family. I also think this is where I developed a nasty habit of coping with conflict. If someone was upset with me or I thought they were, I would go out of my way to try to please them, even giving in and telling them what they wanted to hear or going along with them to keep the peace.

Where most families would come together at the dinner table to share their days, not us. We were not allowed to speak at the dinner table, and God forbid you made a noise eating your food. That was cause for a backhander from him. On one occasion my brother was biting his fork and my sister kicked him under the table. All hell broke loose when my dad saw them misbehaving, and they got sent to their rooms with no supper. This always confused us because when we didn't get sent to our rooms, we were forced to eat everything on our plate, even if we didn't like it or were full. If we didn't like it and my father was sitting at the table watching us, both my brother and I would load the piece of meat, which tasted like shoe leather, with ketchup, so that it could slide down our throats easier. He would make us sit there until 9:00 or 10:00 p.m. until we finally finished every morsel. Our mother used to walk by the table occasionally, and when my dad was not looking, she would eat a piece of whatever it was that we did not want.

I remember one time I was sitting there, and it was getting late, and I was tired. I decided to wrap up all my potatoes in my napkin and put them in my pocket. I then told my dad I was finished, and I was allowed to leave the table. I could not believe this worked. I would continue to employ this tactic often. I even perfected it by putting food in my pockets, right in front of everyone. Nobody ever saw me. Then I would ask to go to the bathroom and flush whatever disgusting food we were having down the toilet. If I didn't have pockets, or they were already full, I used to take peas and hide them under the rim of my dinner plate. When you took the plate away from the table, there was a perfect circle of peas just waiting for my mom to sweep them up and put them in the garbage without my father ever knowing.

Now I can look back and laugh, but it was not so funny then. I swear that is why my brother and I smother everything in ketchup, even to this day.

I do not know exactly what my dad's childhood was like, but he was not a happy man. Often, I wondered if he cared about anyone but himself. Maybe his childhood memories haunted him and made him a drunk, like me. What I do know is that, like me, my father abused alcohol to create a false sense of happiness. He could never just have one drink. He would drink until supper was ready. Once supper was on the table, he would quit drinking for the day and normally pass out immediately after dinner, if he did not pass out before dinner. It was no wonder my mom always had dinner on the table at exactly 5:00 p.m. His drink of choice was rye whiskey with little to no mix, especially after the first couple went down range. The drunker he got, the stronger his poured drinks became. The worst part was that he was a mean drunk. Though he drank excessively, it was kidney disease, not liver disease, that took him. Unfortunately, I inherited many of his traits and very few of my mother's. Unlike him, I didn't stop drinking when supper was on the table. I stopped drinking when the bottle was empty.

Today, as I embark on this long journey of self-healing, I find it very hard to face the fact that my own father, who was supposed to love and protect me, would hurt me both physically and mentally. The constant belittling and abuse made me either want to fight, because I have difficulty controlling my emotions, take flight, because I felt like I was worthless, or simply freeze, because I didn't know what to say or do to make the situation safe for myself.

They say that opposites attract, but my mother and him were more than just opposites. I could never understand why she stayed with him. Just as I could never understand why my wife stayed with me through the years. My mother and my wife are so giving and caring, always putting others before themselves, and he and I only ever thought about ourselves.

Even when my mom was dying of cancer, he still only ever thought about himself. The day the ambulance came to take her to hospice, my father was nowhere to be found. Apparently, he was more worried about telling the neighbours that they were going to hospice than comforting his wife. I arrived at my parents' house in Prince George, BC, the very next morning. They had moved to Prince George from Trenton in 1989, when my dad retired. My sister called to let me know that if I wanted to see Mom, I had better get there quick. I arrived the next morning and my mom asked me what I was doing there. I responded, "I heard you wanted me to come for a visit." She said she didn't want to be a burden and that I had not needed to come. Even to the very end, she put others before herself.

My mother never came home from hospice, and our lives were changed forever. She was our matriarch, our rock, and the one who held our family together through the good times, and most especially, the bad. She always rolled with the punches, just like she taught my wife to do. By the time the cancer took her, she had battled for eight long years, although I am sure they were probably short years to her. She fought breast cancer, then lung cancer, but it was brain cancer that got her in the end. When she died, she had twenty-one tumours in her brain, some the size of golf balls.

Her hardest fight came in hospice those last couple days of her life, but she got the last laugh when she was called home. For days my sister kept telling her that my brother's birthday was coming up; she knew my mom would not want to die on that day. On May 22, 2012, we were celebrating his birthday at hospice. My mom tried to stay awake most of the day, and she even had a bit of cake and kissed her son. While we were wrapping up our celebrations, my father said to us that he did not want to be in the room with her when she took her last breath.

On May 23, the day after my brother's fifty-second birthday, I left hospice and went for a run. Shortly after I left, my siblings went to the front lobby of hospice to work on the puzzle that was used as a distraction for family members. As it was recounted to me, within minutes, my dad came running down the hallway saying, "I think she's dead." My siblings had to practically carry him back to my mom's room. Although barely conscious, she waited until all her children were out of the room and only her husband remained — and she took her last breath. I believe she made a deal with God, in that if she could stay on this earth one last day for her son, then she would go with him the next day. She fought so hard to stay with us for that day, and she kept her word to the big guy.

On May 23, 2012, heaven received a special angel named Betty. I knew the minute I walked back into hospice that my mom had died because I saw the candle burning in the lobby, which meant someone's soul was transitioning to heaven. I got to her room, and they were all standing there. I hugged my mother and kissed her goodbye. I went out into the lobby to call my wife when my dad came out and said, "Okay, Nicki, lets go, I'm ready." Like he was the only one that mattered, like he was the only one allowed to grieve. I replied, "Goddamn it, she wasn't just your wife, she was my mother too. Give me a minute to grieve with Judi and my girls, who just lost their grandmother." I went home with my dad and drank myself into a stupor lying in my mom's bed. I couldn't help thinking, why her and not him! I was angry. I was angry at my father for being such a lousy husband for their entire marriage. I was so angry at my mother's doctor for missing the fact that my mom had pneumonia for three years in a row after having a mastectomy. Had he done his job, they may have found that the cancer had metastasized to her lungs long before it was too late. However, mostly I was mad at God for taking her so soon. Her death made me question my faith in him.

The day following my mother's passing, my dad had me calling

Service Canada, Canada Revenue Agency, and other places to notify them of her death. Imagine the shock in their voices when they asked when she died and I said, "Yesterday!" I was embarrassed and devastated all at the same time. I had lost my mother, and he would not even give me twenty-four hours to mourn her loss before making sure all his tasks were checked off his to-do list!

I spent another week there before it was time for me to leave Prince George and go back to work. I needed an original death certificate so I could claim my expenses for travel. The military will pay for your flight and other minor expenses if you lose an immediate family member, but you must provide proof of the death. My father charged me twenty-five dollars for an original death certificate because he needed the free ones he got, and if he gave me one, he would have to buy another one. I almost threw the money in his face.

My father passed away thirteen months later from kidney failure. My parents had been married for fifty-three years, and for almost all that time he had made her life a living hell. The last couple of years, when her cancer battle got difficult, he simply failed to show up. In fact, he hid in the basement. It was my sister who became my mom's primary caregiver. Without my sister, my mom would never have made it as long as she did. I never forgave him for that. To this day I have never shed a tear over his death.

Having a tumultuous relationship with a parent or even both parents is not unusual. After all, they are only human, subject to the same feelings and imperfections as the rest of us. But there is an enormous difference between typical family bickering and outright toxic behaviour. You do not fully realize it when you are always in the middle of it because you normalize the behaviour. However, as I grew up, I became more aware of how self-centred my father was. Regrettably, having watched him put priority on his needs over those of his children and his wife and all of us having endured physical, verbal, and emotional abuse at his hand, it was hard not to feel trapped. And as a child, it was hard to recognize that these behaviours were not normal. Outbursts and bad days were commonplace, and I learned to blame myself for his behaviours. I thought he acted this way because he was ashamed of me. The guilt and inadequateness I felt as a child followed me into adulthood and made it extremely hard to form normal healthy relationships, taking on what should have been his guilt. I set myself up for the same formula in the CAF, where I took on the guilt for my sexual assault and the guilt for not performing well enough, so I falsely believed the micro-aggressions and men discounting me were warranted. What I didn't know until very recently was that I was suffering from complex trauma, which was affecting my development and sense of safety in the world.

Thank God I married someone just like my mother because she is still with me, despite all I have put her through, even allowing my father's trauma to infect me and then becoming part of a system that perpetuates it. I was a loose cannon when it came to my emotions, and she never knew what was going to set me off. Both my spouse and my children walked around on eggshells. Judi told me once that she was having a heart-to-heart with my mother, who told her that marriage was hard but once you committed you stayed and put in the hard work, and you learned to roll with the punches. My mother knew what it was like to be married to a military member, and I was more like my father than I cared to admit. I mimicked the behaviour I witnessed from my father as a child, but recently, thanks to the help of my clinical psychologist, I recognized that as an adult I have choices that I didn't have growing up. If I wanted to be the person I see inside my mind's eye, I needed to change and put in a herculean effort to make these character improvements. This doctor changed my life.

Since the death of our parents, my siblings and I are closer than we have ever been. We are truly getting to know each other as people. It has been one of the greatest feelings of my life. I did not realize how much I loved them until I really got to know them as human beings and friends.

3
Recruit Course 8746 - Ready Aye Ready

You don't lose if you get knocked down; you lose if you stay down.
— *Muhammad Ali*

IT WAS JUNE 15, 1984, the day after I graduated from Loyalist College of Applied Arts and Technology. I was twenty-one years old, and my father reluctantly drove me to the Recruiting Centre in Peterborough, Ontario, where I tried to enlist in the Canadian Armed Forces (CAF). He knew what I would be subjected to as he had served the Royal Canadian Navy from 1968 until 1984. What he didn't understand was that my experience of basic training would be so much worse than his, simply because I was a woman.

Back then, the goal of basic recruit training was to break you down as individuals so the system could rebuild you into what they were looking for; to strip you of your individualism only to build you back up again as a team. And because individuals have an innate desire to belong, the CAF uses the forming, norming, storming, conforming, performing stages of team development to begin the socialization into the CAF culture.

In my opinion, the most important stage for the CAF is that of conformity, which is regulated by military authority in the form of rank. The other thing that conformity does is to get people to mould their beliefs, attitudes, actions, and perceptions to more closely match those held by the group to which they belong or want to belong or by groups whose approval they seek. This is the beginning of how power is absorbed, shaped, and distributed across the organization.

The bottom line is that heterosexual white males are set up for success right out of the gate, while most females are destined to always take a backseat or play a secondary supporting role. There is the odd female who will make it to the very top, such as Christine Whitecross did when she was appointed as the first female three-star general. She was also the first female and only the third Canadian Armed Forces member to be appointed as the commandant of the North Atlantic Treaty Organization (NATO) Defence College. As a trailblazer, she had many, many other firsts beyond the two I just listed. LGen Whitecross was an amazing leader, and regardless of how busy she was, she always took the time to speak with you and offer advice if asked. She inspired a new generation of trailblazers.

My father and I left our home in Trenton very early that morning and arrived at the recruiting centre in Peterborough just as the recruiter was unlocking the front door. We walked inside, and I quickly learned that the Military Police (MP) occupation was not taking any applicants. Unfathomable! The trade was closed. The recruiter tried to get me to choose something else, but I would not, so I wrote MP, MP, MP for each of the choices they gave me. Before leaving there I faced my first major moral dilemma when the recruiter asked if I was a homosexual. Do I lie and go against every moral fibre of my being, or do I tell the truth and give up on my lifelong dream because society thinks I suffer from a character flaw and am not worthy of serving my country? I went against everything my mother had taught me — in that moment I lied, cheated, and stole. I lied to the recruiter, I cheated the recruitment system, and I stole a heterosexual identity, all for the honour of serving Canada. In that one fatal moment I completely lost myself as a person. I had sinned, and it would be the first of so many more sins to come. But I had been lying since I was five years old and hadn't yet realized that I was lying to myself as well. I was hiding who I really was.

That summer after I finished college, I would check the mail every day hoping I would find a letter from the CAF in the mailbox, telling me I was now accepted as a member. But as the days turned into weeks, and the weeks into months, and finally the months to years, I had almost given up hope. I had to wait three and a half years before I heard from the CAF. My God, I got a post-secondary diploma quicker than it took the CAF to recruit me. As the days passed by, I became less and less confident and more and more scared. Then I would get mad. Had the recruiter somehow guessed that I was a homosexual? I was making myself sick with worry and driving Tracy crazy. I think she was happier than I was when I opened my letter of acceptance. Finally, I was accepted. I was going to be a member of the Canadian Armed Forces. I could not contain my excitement! Normally, I would have been considered old for a recruit at age of twenty-four, but the average age of our cohort was twenty-three years of age due to one recruit, who was forty-four years old. We had one individual who was under the age of eighteen, and who had to have her parents sign a waiver to allow her to enroll in the CAF.

As happy as I was to finally get the "nod," I was also very sad to be leaving my military girlfriend of four years. Tracy and I met on the baseball diamond. She was playing for the military team and I was playing for a civilian team in the same league as the military team. We started dating in 1983, a year before I finished college, and we moved in together in 1984, the year I graduated from Loyalist College of Applied Arts. Ours was always a rocky relationship, but I think because she was my first real love, she had a strange hold on me that I could not break. I thought it was love, but upon reflection she had something I desperately wanted: a career in the Canadian Armed Forces.

In November 1987, I was off to Cornwallis. The drive from Chilliwack to the Vancouver airport normally took around one hour and thirty minutes. When you want time to slow down, it is almost mind boggling how fast it flies by. Not a lot was said between Tracy and I as the miles clicked by. Both of us were lost in our own thoughts. We decided that she would drop me off in front of the airport and then Tracy would head back to the home we shared in Chilliwack, which we had moved into in July 1987 after Tracy was told she would be leaving her post in Trenton with a posting to Chilliwack and a promotion to the rank of Warrant Officer (WO).

As we got closer to the airport, I was reconsidering our decision to not have a long goodbye. We had said our tear-stained goodbyes the night before while making plans for me to come home for Christmas and for her to attend my graduation.

As Tracy pulled up to the curb in the front of the airport, I didn't want to get out of the passenger seat. Despite wanting to serve my country, to join the CAF so I could live my career within my calling, to defend my country, uphold its ideals, regulations, and principles, I did not want to leave this woman, but I had no choice. I had wanted to serve my country since before I could properly formulate sentences and I was not giving up that dream. I finally got out of the car; Tracy left, and I reluctantly entered the airport.

I boarded the military flight bound for Halifax, where a bus would then transport us to CFB Cornwallis. The flight seemed to take forever because it stopped in every city across Canada to pick up people. I would come to learn that this was what the military called the "Milk Run." When the flight landed in Halifax, gone was Nicki Belanger, and I was transformed into Private Basic (Pte) (B) Belanger, 862. My life was about to change forever because I made a choice to join an organization that didn't want me for two reasons: I was a homosexual and female. For most of my career, I was never sure what the greater sin was — being a woman or being gay.

Upon arrival in Halifax, we were all ushered onto the bus that would take us to Cornwallis, the English-speaking division of the Canadian Forces Leadership and Recruit School for the entire Canadian Forces on land, sea, and air. I immediately felt like I had come home. It was a nice, quiet bus ride, but as soon as we arrived on the base and got off the bus, strange men in various coloured uniforms started barking commands at us. I was literally twitching with excitement. I had watched the military operate from the periphery and hung around military folks all my life, so the uniforms, the strange men yelling at us was all too familiar. Not to mention that when I found out I would be going to Cornwallis, Tracy gave me a crash course in the various rank structures, how to salute, and how to do basic drill movements. When one of the instructors yelled for us to form up in three ranks, I jumped and got on the line. Nobody else moved an inch. It became readily apparent that only I knew what form up meant. I was so eager to please and show off what I knew that I immediately got noticed. Apparently, this was not a good thing in Cornwallis.

The Master Seaman (MS) came storming up to me and asked my name. I quickly stood to attention and smartly responded, "Belanger, Master Seaman." Another mistake!

"Do you have previous military experience, Belanger?"

"No, Master Seaman."

"Do you have cadet experience, Belanger?"

"No, Master Seaman."

"Were you in Girl Guides, Belanger?"

"No, Master Seaman."

"Boy Scouts?"

At this point I started to panic and managed to stammer "No, Master Seaman." I began to feel an uncomfortable pit in the bottom of my stomach.

"Then, how the hell do you know my rank? Get down and give me twenty-five." He was referring to push-ups, and I would do many, many more of them before escaping Cornwallis.

Ours was one of the first platoons to go through Cornwallis that combined men and women together. We all lived in the same barrack or housing block and received the same training. We were course 8746. There were eighteen women in my platoon and only two of us women were going through to be Military Police (MP). Pte Vivian House was from a small village in Newfoundland, and we naturally bonded. Viv, I would come to learn, had a bachelor's degree in social work, and the recruiter told her to enlist as a MP because they did similar things to social workers. Boy, was she in for a surprise! Oh, and she only had to wait two weeks to get her letter of offer. I asked all the potential male recruits going through to be MP how long they had to wait. The longest wait out of the sixteen of them was ten days, compared to my three-and-a-half-year wait.

On the first official training day of recruit school, we were marched over to the barber shop to get our haircuts. No salon for the girls, just the barber, and we all got the same haircut, unless you wanted to wear it in a bun every day. This was just one more way to enforce the masculine culture of the military. From there we were fitted for our uniforms. I had waited for this day all my life. I could hardly contain myself. I secretly used to try on Tracy's uniforms while she was at work, just to get a feel for what it would eventually be like to be a member of the profession of arms. I was trembling with excitement. I was about to legitimately get my very own uniforms, tailor made and properly sized for me!

I lined up in alphabetical order with all my platoon mates and patiently waited my turn to be issued everything that I would need over the next thirteen weeks. It didn't take long before I was at the front of the line.

"What size are your feet, recruit?"

"Size three and a half, sir."

"First, do not call me 'sir,' I work for a living," he screamed at me. "Second, we do not have boots that small. Here is a size five. Make it work." Seeing me hesitate, he shouted, "What are you waiting for, get the hell out of here!"

I then moved to the uniform line where I was given my designated environmental uniform (DEU), my DEU shirts, and my Canadian Forces belt. While waiting for the rest of my equipment and clothing, I found myself examining my military belt. My mind drifted back to my dad and how he used his military belt to beat my sister, brother, and I. That black leather military belt with brass buckle was just a belt to hold up pants to the other recruits, but to me it was much more than that. It might as well have been a rifle, as it was just as dangerous when in my father's hands.

I didn't give much thought to the remainder of military kit I received, but later realized that every piece of kit I was issued was either too big or too small; I would just have to make do. My bowler (hat for DEU with jacket and medals) was too small, my wedge cap (hat for DEU without medals or DEU short-sleeve shirt, no jacket) was too big, my tunic fit more like a short blazer, not even covering my bum. My combat jacket and parka were all too big. In fact, I never had to wear gloves in the winter because my jacket sleeves were way longer than my arms. So much for having my own uniforms that were properly sized for me!

Not even the military belt could compare to the worst piece of kit I was issued, which was my green one-piece Speedo swimsuit. As a competitive swimmer I was not used to having my breasts pop out the sides of my suit every time I dove in the water. As you can imagine, it significantly slowed me down when I had to stop and put each breast back in my suit before I could start swimming. My running shoes were a green canvas, but unfortunately, they were too big, so I had to wear two pairs of white sport socks and a pair of grey wool socks in them. The military were not yet equipped or ready for shorter-statured individuals entering the Force. There was no such thing as gender-based analysis back then. Oh, and who can forget my shorts, which came up to just below my breasts! That was okay because my T-shirt had a plunging neckline that tucked into my shorts. I was not winning any beauty pageants, that was for sure. I often wondered how anyone got laid in Cornwallis looking like that, but they did. The lack of a proper kit for female recruits was rather telling that the CAF did not care to have women amongst them.

That evening, after returning to our barracks with all our new clothes, we had a chance to introduce ourselves to each other. It was at this point that I learned that Master Corporal (MCpl) Patricia Perrin would be our platoon instructor. Pat was my next-door neighbour from Trenton and someone I played softball against. She and I had often joked that it would be funny if I ended up in her platoon when I finally got accepted into the CAF. The reality was not as funny as we originally thought. Pat was stuck between a rock and a hard place by me showing up. If she admitted that she knew me they could recourse me, but if she lied or simply ignored it and they found out, it would be even worse. She told her Warrant Officer that she knew me, and I was allowed to continue, but both her and I were under close scrutiny for fraternization.

If that was not bad enough, when I walked into weapons class, there was my girlfriend's ex-lover, whom I had met and partied with several times. She was going to be teaching me weapons handling. I had to pretend I didn't know her. It was hard using her rank as opposed to her first name, like I had done for the past three years that I had known her. No sooner did I get over that encounter when I ran into a friend who I used to go running with all the time in Trenton, before Tracy and I moved to Chilliwack. I thought he was still in Trenton; I had no idea he was posted to Cornwallis. This took me by surprise. He came up to my table at lunch and said to me, "Eat all your vegetables, Private, or else I will tell your mother." I retorted, "Fuck you, Master Seaman," before I could think about what I was saying. All the other recruits at my table sucked in their breath and held it, waiting for the backlash. Paul simply laughed and walked over to his own platoon and started to yell at them to hurry up. I think that was the first and last time that a fuck-you ever gave me "street cred" right off the bat!

After the initial excitement of being in Cornwallis wore off, the days started to run into one another, and the only way to gauge which day was which was to recall the shit you got in that day. For example, I had left my novel out after a weekend and MCpl Perrin came in and found it. This was a "no-no" as all personal stuff was to have already been put away in our foot lockers. I immediately owned up to the fact that it was my book. MCpl Perrin assigned me a minor punishment of fifty push-ups. I got down in the prone position and completed my first push-up. MCpl Perrin then left and walked into the washroom. I quickly sat up and continued to count as if I was still doing push-ups. When I got to forty-eight, I assumed the push-up position and yelled out forty-nine. MCpl Perrin came out of the washroom. She asked the platoon, "Does everyone think Pte Belanger has had enough?" One woman said, "No, Master Corporal." This female, who went by the name Pte Hamilton, happened to be the seventeen-year-old, the youngest member of course 8746. She was going through for a Navy trade. MCpl Perrin gave me twenty-five more push-ups, and this time she stayed to watch. After I completed the twenty-five push ups, MCpl Perrin left for the night and I bee-lined it to this Private. I was seething. I promptly told this youngster that I would ensure that I was either the Course Senior or the Squad Senior for the rest of the time we would be in Cornwallis and that I would go out of my way to make certain that she got every dirty job I could imagine. I kept my word, and she performed some shitty jobs during the last five weeks of training.

Another time, I learned that Pte Hamilton was the one who was going into the storage unit after we all went to bed and using the cleaning products and supplies and not tidying up after. The storage room was Vivian's job, and she would clean it before bedtime. She never bothered to check it in the morning, thinking everything was fine. Little did Vivian know that this young woman was making a mess in there and then would simply walk away. I was tired of seeing Vivian get in trouble every time we had an inspection because of her, so I thought I would teach her a lesson. I emptied a whole can of spray starch on her shoes, which happened to be sitting right near my ironing board. Her shoes were never the same after that little warning shot. She knew I did it, but she never said a word about that, nor did she ever tell on me. While this may not have been the right thing to do, it was considered an example of barrack room justice for someone who is consistently not team player.

To say that I was a little cocky was an understatement. Tracy and some others training me in the basics was not necessarily the best thing they could have done for me. Instead of using this knowledge to share, help, and inspire other women in my squad, I used it to my own personal advantage, and it showed. An example of this was when I decided that the ladies who were having a hard time with certain drill movements required extra training in the barrack block room, whether they wanted to partake or not. This carried on for weeks before one of the ladies squealed to the instructors. MCpl Perrin put a stop to it immediately. She was not pleased with me, and I felt terrible because I always wanted to please her.

    These women were all afraid of me, and I thought that was a good thing because my father had taught me that if people disliked you then you were doing your job properly. Clearly, my parental conditioning was coming into focus during my indoctrination into the CAF. In fact, I would say that indoctrination methods did not work with me because I got indoctrinated while I was a teenager in Trenton by associating with military personnel. So, the Cornwallis method had no sway on me. I was privileged by my prior experience.

    On another day, we got dressed in the morning and someone forgot to centre off their boots — taking whatever pair of boots that corresponded with the uniform we were wearing that day down from the top of our locker and centre off the other pairs of footwear that remained. The instructor cadre came in and threw all our boots into the centre of the platoon room. We had to find our boots and put them back on the top of our lockers where they belonged. This was like trying to find a needle in a haystack because everyone had the same boots and shoes. This is where having small feet paid off. I walked into the centre of the pile, found my plastic high-heeled dress boots, picked up my tiny dress shoes, and located the smallest pair of rubber gummies (over-boots) that were in the pile and returned to my bedspace. Some people spent more than an hour looking for their footwear. We never made that mistake again.

    On one particular morning, someone had given me a chocolate bar because I had not had time for breakfast. I was too busy getting ready for an inspection of our military kit and bedspaces to eat it right away. While I was dismantling my weapon and lining the pieces up on my bed, making sure that they were all centred on the black stripe of my wool blanket, I laid my chocolate bar down as well and then promptly forgot it there. MCpl Perrin marched in and started to inspect my bedspace and then asked me if I was trying to bribe her.

I conducted a sharp about-turn and there was MCpl Perrin pointing to the chocolate bar, centred on the black stripe of my wool blanket. After she repeated her question, I replied, "No, Master Corporal, unless it would work." With a little smirk on her face, she said, "No, it will not," walked out of my bedspace, and carried on with her inspection on the next unsuspecting recruit. My chocolate bar was in her pocket, and I just knew I was going to be starving by lunchtime!

Each day at Cornwallis, I was in some sort of shit or just getting noticed for all the wrong reasons. Every day for the first three weeks, I found my bed mattress on the ground outside my window on the second floor. When we made our beds, our pillow had to be tucked under the grey wool blanket and had to measure eighteen inches. Seemingly, I didn't know how to measure because at the end of each training day I would pick my mattress off the ground, carry it up a flight of stairs and put it back on my bed.

In 2018, I took my wife, Judi, to Greenwood, Nova Scotia, to celebrate her fiftieth birthday with some of our friends. We took a day trip to Cornwallis. As we drove onto the old base, my mouth went dry and I started to get heart palpitations, almost like I was having a heart attack. We also did a tour of my old barrack block, and I swear to God there was still an outline of a single mattress on the ground below my window. No grass had grown there in thirty years. I took a picture and send it to Pat Perrin with the caption, Guess where I am?

During our fifth week of a thirteen-week training schedule, we were permitted to wear our civilian clothes and go to the Green and Gold, the military's version of a neighbourhood bar. We ran to get our suitcases as we had not seen our civilian clothing since we arrived. We were forced to trade them in for a pair of green coveralls, which we always wore inside our barrack block, along with a soaking wet beret on our heads, so it would form properly. My hair took on that dead rat look. I opened my suitcase, and after much thought selected what I was going to wear on my big night out. I showered and then put on my socks and underwear. When I stood upright my underwear fell right down past my knees. They were now about three sizes too big — I thought they were my mother's! Then I realized that I had lost that much weight. Running everywhere all day, doing thirteen-kilometre marches with a sixty-pound rucksack on your back and not being able to have snack food at night will do that to you.

On December 5, three weeks into my training, I got a surprise: I had received flowers and a card in the mail from Tracy. Since all our incoming and outgoing mail was scrutinized by the staff, MCpl Perrin, thinking these might be from Tracy, used my friendship with Paul, the male Master Seaman (MS) on staff, to protect my real identity and told her peers that if they opened my mail and it was from the MS, they would be forced to report a fellow staff member. Their sense of loyalty to protect one of their own was more important than catching a lesbian. They did not open my mail that day and my secret remained safe for the moment, thanks to MCpl Perrin's quick thinking. This could have been disastrous and when I learned of it, I was shitting bricks. I still have never figured out why Tracy would send me flowers, considering that sometime between November 12 and December 5, 1987, Tracy had managed to find someone to replace me in her life. Just before leaving Cornwallis for Christmas break, she broke up with me and alluded to the fact that we would still be together if I had not gone to Cornwallis. The truth was she had been cheating on me before my airplane landed in Cornwallis. When you call home and a strange woman is answering your phone and it is not your girlfriend, you begin to wonder. And when you call home at 0630 hrs on a Sunday morning and the same woman again answers your phone, it does not take a genius to figure it out, especially when you know the telephone was on your side of the bed when you left!

I went home to my parents' house in Trenton for Christmas Break to lick my wounds since I no longer had a home of my own to go to in Chilliwack. During the holiday I had lots of time to think and I was stupidly considering not going back to Cornwallis so that I could restore my relationship with Tracy. I almost gave up on my dream for this woman. In the end, I voluntarily went back to Cornwallis. Even those who did not know me were asking MCpl Perrin what happened to me over the holidays. I left for Christmas break as a top recruit, and I came back as a slug, according to the male instructors. I managed to finish out the rest of my training, but not without incident.

The mental abuse and harassment at the hands of the recruit instructors did not start right away. It took about a good month before they started to hone in on me. I was called a split-ass and a CUNT for the first time in my life in Cornwallis. Apparently, "CUNT" stands for "cruite" (slang for recruit) under naval training. I could tell that this man was particularly fond of himself as he was laughing at his own witticism. I leaned in and whispered in his ear, "You are a big prick, but you don't hear me saying that, do you?" I spun on my heel and walked away, leaving him to stare after me with mouth agape.

And I will never forget the MCpl who told me that women did not belong in the military. According to him, war fighting was for men and women should just stay home barefoot and pregnant! I recall another instructor coming up to a group of us women one weekend when we were at the Green and Gold and start to carry out a conversation with all of us. It was evident he had had too much to drink. He turned to me and began to ask personal questions of me, such as if I was married. When I replied no, he asked if I had a boyfriend. Again, I replied no, and at this point, in front of my fellow soldiers, he said that it was probably a good thing because I would need to date a faggot so I could be the man in the relationship. I took several deep breaths, swallowed my humiliation, slowly plastered a smile on my face, and then asked if he was volunteering to be my girlfriend. Everyone laughed. I knew this was the wrong thing to do but I just could not help myself.

Other micro-aggressions included sneaking into my bed space and hiding candy in the pocket of my parka. Fortunately for me, I found the candy before the inspection the next morning. I was holding them in my hand when the Petty Officer 2nd Class (PO2) came in and went straight for my parka. He rummaged through my pockets, and I could hear him cursing under his breath when he couldn't locate the candy. I couldn't help myself. When he was leaving my bedspace, I uncurled my fingers, thrust out my hand, and asked him if that was what he was looking for. Needless to say, when his face went beet red, I knew I had, again, unintentionally put another target on my back. It seemed to me that the male instructors would always insult me when MCpl Perrin was not present. I suspect she would have "schooled them on professional conduct" and they wanted no part of that. I also never told her what they were saying and doing.

 I rarely went away on weekends when we were finally allowed to leave the base, but on one weekend I went into Digby and was five minutes late getting back to barracks. All of the instructors were waiting to see if MCpl Perrin was going to punish me, and she did. I was ordered to write "in order to be dependable, one must be in the designated place at the desired time" out one hundred times, which I did, with no help from my friends. The next morning, I handed in my lines and was asked by the PO2 if I learned anything. I replied by saying, "I learned that this was stupid, PO2."

 "At least you learned how to spell dependable and designated."

 "No, I already knew how to spell those big words. I have a college education, PO."

 "Get out of my face, Belanger!"

 I would do stuff like that all the time in Cornwallis, and it was a wonder they ever let me graduate. One time I grabbed two ice cream cups, one for me and one for a guy who had forgotten to grab his. We were only entitled to take one. The MCpl saw me grab two and decided that a good punishment would be to make me run up and down the bleachers during drill class. I did not care because I was in the best shape of my life. As I ran up and down, I was smiling and waving to all the other recruits who were doing drill. The PO told the MCpl to send me back to my platoon as I was making a fool out of him.

 My next close encounter came in February 1988, on the eve of our graduation parade. When I didn't show up at the home I shared with

Tracy for Christmas, she decided she was coming to my graduation, even though we had broken up. It did not matter to her that I was not in a good place emotionally to see her. I was still extremely hurt over our breakup. Back then we had to submit a guest list of people coming and their relationship to us. We told her that she had to have already been on my documents. She wasn't and didn't care, so I put her on them. The other instructors questioned MCpl Perrin about this because Tracy was not originally on my documents as my sister. I unknowingly put MCpl Perrin in a position where she was forced to lie for me.

If that was not bad enough, the evening before the graduation parade, I got caught by the Military Police in the senior non-commissioned officer's (NCO) barrack block. A location that was out of bounds to me. While waiting for Tracy to change out of her uniform, someone knocked on the door. I opened it to find the MP standing there. We must have been followed. They wanted to know why I was in the senior NCO barracks and asked if I knew these quarters were out of bounds. Of course I knew, but I pled ignorance and it seemed to work because the MP did not put me in jail or worse, turn me over to the Special Investigation Unit (SIU) to be interrogated and purged from the CAF. I thought I got away with it and laughed all the way back to MCpl Perrin's house, where we continued our party, away from the prying eyes of the Military Police.

The other good laugh I got that week came when the opportunity presented itself to introduce Tracy to the MCpl who called me a "CUNT" and who liked to tell me that the only place women belonged was in the kitchen, barefoot and pregnant. She was a Warrant Officer (WO) and he a MCpl, meaning she was two ranks higher than he was. I must admit it was vindictive of me, but I just could not resist. After introducing him to her, I walked away, silently laughing, while she had a chat with him about respect. Then I sat at a nearby table and watched. It was like watching a car crash — you know you shouldn't look but you just can't help yourself.

This MCpl was most likely a product of his environment, and he was just repeating what he had learned his entire life. Women had never really been accepted into the military, and for the government to ask a long-standing institution such as the Canadian Armed Forces to hire more women was like asking the Shriner's to let women join the fraternity. It just was not going to happen without a lot of feet dragging on the part of the military.

The culture between the 1970 and 1989 was one of individualism, careerism, and deceit, and as such, the senior leaders of the CAF refused gender integration. Without leadership buy-in there was little to no monitoring of gender integration implementation. The male leaders refused to believe that women could also be very good at war, as that was believed to be the restricted purview of men. The next ten years (1989–1999), coined as the "Decade of Darkness," did not help the cause of women either. In fact, the Decade of Darkness didn't help anyone in the CAF. Good news for women in the military and those wishing to join came in 1985 when section 15 of the Canadian Charter of Rights and Freedoms came into effect; however, the CAF still managed to drag their feet, not rushing to open all occupations to women despite being ordered to by the new Charter. It wasn't until 2001 before every occupation in the CAF was open to women, including submarine service in the Royal Canadian Navy. However, just because all occupations were now open to women, that did not automatically mean that women were accepted. From 1999 onward, the toxicity level didn't change much from the previous twenty years, and diversity, equity, and inclusivity were not yet the buzzwords they are today.

Those last few days in Cornwallis were both frustrating and scary at the same time. Misogyny was alive and well. I was informed that no "split-ass" was going to be the top student of a naval platoon, even though I had earned that distinction. I was also notified that because I was a smoker, I could not be the top athlete of my recruit class, even though I had earned that too. MCpl Perrin fought hard for me and even tried to get me a small parade position, but in the end, it did not matter how good I was, they would never let me forget that I was a woman! I would be like all the other women, in amongst the men, in the ranks and not standing out front or even having a parade position for guests to see. Many times throughout recruit school I felt like a little lab rat, with all eyes on me, watching me scurry about in my cage, hoping I would fall off the hamster wheel and reveal myself for exactly what I was.

While I thought I had gotten away with being found in the senior NCO barracks, the misdeed had not been forgotten, as I had hoped it would be. The morning of our graduation parade, I had to answer to the Commandant. I was escorted to his office where I again pled ignorance and MCpl Perrin again saved me. She vouched for me to the Commandant. I could and would graduate. It was in that moment when I realized the true importance of needing to learn how to hide in plain sight. I could not escape Cornwallis fast enough. There was an inconsistency in the messages I was receiving. Were they targeting me because their Spidey-senses were telling them that I was a homosexual or were they trying to get me to quit because of gender stereotypes? Was the crime being a homosexual or simply being a woman? What I do know is that they tried extremely hard to knock me down and keep me there, but there was no way I was staying down, especially with great leaders like MCpl Perrin supporting me from behind. I had wanted this too much to allow some bully to intimidate me into quitting.

I will forever be indebted to MCpl Perrin for saving my career while I underwent training. She was an amazing leader who demonstrated empathy, confidence, and most importantly, professionalism. She went the extra mile for all her recruits. While I did not know it at the time, MCpl Perrin had become my first role model and mentor in the CAF. Throughout my career I found myself fashioning my leadership style based on the example she set. I thought if I could be half the leader she was, I would be highly successful in my career. Every time I got knocked down in my career, I symbolically felt her gentle hands guiding me back to my feet, telling me to get up, dust myself off, and to keep fighting. I was so very blessed when I retired to have her at my Change of Appointment ceremony. It was such an honour for me to share this occasion with her. If not for her protection in recruit school and the leadership lessons she imparted on me, I probably would not have made it to the rank I retired from. The woman who saw me come into the CAF also watched me leave the CAF.

4
The Impact of Trauma

You wake up every morning to fight the same demons that left you so tired the night before, and that, my love, is bravery.
— *Unknown*

I WAS FOOLISH ENOUGH TO THINK that this hidden hatred of women and other diverse groups would disappear as soon as I left a training environment such as Cornwallis. I thought that once we all earned our spot by going through an identical experience and wearing the same uniform for our country that we would all be considered equal. I soon realized how wrong I was.

It wasn't long before that pure and open hatred started to show itself. I don't blame these women. They conformed by adapting a male misogynistic identity. What they did was no different than me adapting a male leadership model to advance through the ranks.

What's more, I did such a good job as a recruit in Cornwallis that all the male instructors thought I was a Special Investigations Unit (SIU) member who was sent there to observe any inappropriate behaviour by the staff members. According to MCpl Perrin, who recounted this story to me much later in our careers, she didn't help matters when, shortly after our course graduated and she took her leave and came back to Cornwallis, she told them that she saw me in uniform in Trenton, and that I was a Sgt! They all started to scamper like cockroaches when you turn the light on in a dark room! I have no idea if they ever figured out that I was not an SIU plant. I only wish I could have been a fly on the wall when MCpl Perrin told them. I bet the MCpl who called me a CUNT experienced a little tightening of his sphincter when he heard I might be SIU. She never did tell them the truth, and for those who broke the coveted trust the system put in them to lead a future generation of soldiers, I hope it always remained in the back of their minds. It certainly stayed with me for my entire career and into retirement.

During MP training we had to take basic typing. We had an instructor who used to tell us to sit down and shut our fucking mouths before we even came into the typing classroom. One day she sprang on us that we were going to have a typing test. My desk partner was Cpl Taylor, who typed about ten words a minute compared to my forty words per minute. Before the test began, Pte House was having a problem with her keys sticking, so I went to see if I could help her. While I was doing this, Cpl Taylor typed his name on my paper and hid it under the platen, or the roller bar of the typewriter. I sat back down, and the test began. Not even one minute into the test and my paper got ripped out of my typewriter. I whipped around and said, "What the fuck!" The typing instructor was standing behind me, gripping my paper and shaking it at me for all she was worth. "You little cheater," she kept hissing at me as spittle ran down her double chin. I was trying to remain respectful, but she kept telling me to shut my fucking mouth. And then she called me a "snot-nose little no-hook Private." Cpl Taylor was trying to explain that he did it as a joke and that I did not know he had done it. She told him to shut his mouth and then kicked everyone out of the classroom except me. After trying to speak and being constantly interrupted and being called a "snot-nose little no-hook Private" a second time I'd had enough. Something in me snapped at that moment, and I was immediately transported back to my childhood with my father standing there berating me. I calmly walked over and closed the classroom door, walked back to her, and said, "You listen here, you fat fucking cow, I told you I did not cheat. If you want to charge me, go ahead!" I spun on my heels and walked out. I finally got the courage to talk back to someone in authority.

The school Regimental Sergeant-Major (RSM) was the lead

investigator in the case against me. At the end of his investigation, and after he interrogated both Cpl Taylor and I, he told us that we were either the best liars he had ever met or else we were telling the truth. I don't know about Cpl Taylor, but I was the queen of lying. I had been lying my entire life! Only this time I was telling the truth. How ironic — when I lied, people believed me, but when I told the truth, no one believed me.

It did not seem to matter that there was no proof that I intended to cheat or that Cpl Taylor admitted to being the one who typed his name on my paper. I was charged anyway! At that point in our careers, I was no less qualified to become a military police officer than he was, yet the system was still willing to sacrifice me to save his career, even though he confessed to the crime.

The system of patriarchy is designed to shift blame, where women are responsible for the crime regardless of the evidence put in front of the organization. If you think back to the when we first started experiencing a crisis in our culture concerning sexual misconduct, we did the exact same thing. We blamed women for the actions of men. This is known in psychology as the "just-world phenomenon," which is the tendency to believe that the world is just and that people get what they deserve. Based on this phenomenon, who did I think I was, trying to join a very male-dominated occupation that was rife with male cognitive biases that distort the institution's thinking!

It felt like the house (MP leadership) made a calculated bet that this particular male's potential would outweigh my performance and therefore concluded that he would be the more productive member of the Profession of Arms (POA). He was a good person. I do not know why he pulled the plug early on his career, but I did hear that he'd had enough of the double standards at the time. For example, the preponderance of operators in command positions, the perceived privileged advantage that Army personnel had over others, and the fact that female standards for the PT test seemed too low compared to male standards.

Whether his perceptions were valid or not is another story. I agreed with him that at one time in the not-so-distant past, physical fitness standards for women were low, but at least the EXPRES test actually measured your physical fitness level and not just your brute strength like the FORCE test. The philosophy is that "same" means that two or more things are exactly alike, while "equal" means that two or more things are functionally equivalent but they are not exactly alike. This new test followed the Canadian Charter of Rights and Freedoms, which has specific instructions to establish a bona fide occupational requirement (BFOR). I cannot speak for the entire female population of the CAF, but I can tell you that this test was brutal. I began doing the FORCE test in 2012, which was the introductory year. I hurt my back every time I took the test because the weights were simply too heavy for a person my size (five foot one and 135 pounds). Doing the shuttle run or lifting a 40-pound sandbag onto your shoulder and then walking the width of the gym five times is not that hard, but lifting 40-pound sandbags thirty times and having to lift it up to a certain height and then finishing the test by dragging a 240-pound "sandbag man" the width of the gym is not fun, especially when you only weigh 135 pounds. Today, you cannot throw a needle at my back and not hit some part of it that has not been damaged from doing that test. I have been diagnosed with angular fractures, compressed fractures, bulging discs, bones spurs on my spine, and severe osteoarthritis.

We do need gender standards for physical fitness. We are built differently. We are not the same, but rather we are equal. In the case of Cpl Taylor, the house would have lost their shirt on the bet as he finished his career early and at the rank of Sergeant.

5

Locked in My Cage with Guilt and Shame

The hardest prison to escape is the one in our mind.
— *Unknown*

AS A MILITARY POLICEWOMAN I naively thought that being in a position of power, having a badge and a gun, would afford me protection against misogynistic attitudes. It didn't. In fact, it made me more of a target. Society made me believe that sexually inappropriate behaviours, including assaults and harassments perpetrated against me, were somehow my fault. If I complained that you, a senior non-commissioned member, offered to give me the posting of my choice if I gave you a blowjob, I would be labelled as a squealer, and you would be patted on the back by your buddies or even better, promoted and posted. Your overall impression of me and others like me was that I lacked the military ethos, that I did not possess the same core values as other CAF members.

Now, I can admit to myself, after having travelled this long and extremely difficult path and received extensive cognitive behavioural therapy, that not only do I possess a sense of duty, but I am loyal and my integrity is unquestionable. What can be questioned is my courage. I lacked the courage to report you. Instead, I shoved the hurt so far down inside me and pretended it didn't happen. I did not want to be the person who was put on trial, to protect my career, so I said nothing. This is why so many people stay silent. To come forward and report would put a person's reputation in the crosshairs — subject to judgment. My confidence in the system's ability to judge fairly is the calculus that I based my decision on, not the circumstances of the event. As a MP I too often watched the military courts fail to protect victims, and I even watched my own trade fail to protect MP victims. The message was clear: complain and we will get rid of you; keep your mouth shut and we just might allow you to serve at our pleasure.

The night you, my peer, decided that it was your God-given right to pin me up against that dark and dingy wall at the corner bar and whisper in my ear that "You were going to fuck the gay out of me" was the night you robbed me of any self-esteem I had left. I thought that you grinding your penis into my crotch was the worst thing I had ever experienced until you tried to force your tongue into my mouth. I had to swallow the bile that immediately rose up at the smell of your disgusting garlic breath. To this day, I cannot kiss my wife if she has eaten garlic, nor can I be near anyone who has garlic breath. As soon as I smell it on someone's breath, I think of you and I begin to gag and want to vomit.

My greatest desire is that you are reading this book and it makes you feel terrible. I pray that you have a daughter who grows up to realize she is a lesbian. I hope your love for her overcomes your bigotry. I hope that it forces you to realize how inappropriate, and in fact criminal, your behaviour toward me was that night. There is no excuse for what you did to me. If you have brushed this behaviour off as a drunken incident or have completely put it out of your mind as inconsequential, to never be thought of again, you have no regard for the significance of this incident. I wasn't able to put it out of my mind, in fact I think about it most days, and for the longest time society helped convince me that it was my fault.

As a result, for almost thirty years I kept your secret, thinking it was my shame to hide. I kept this secret not because I wanted to but because I knew that the military didn't want me to talk about it. I thought that keeping this secret would make me safer, but I was wrong. I now know that secrets are deadly freight.

At first, I felt guilty for having gone to that bar and having gotten drunk. Later, the shame set in, and I actually felt for a time that I deserved it because of being gay. In Daring Greatly, Brené Brown says that guilt is a mistake whereas shame says I am the mistake, and that shame is more powerful than guilt because it strikes at your identity. You are the one who should be ashamed of what you did, but because of the way our toxic military culture viewed gender-based violence, I had no choice but to keep that secret on your behalf. Every secret I was forced to keep, every insult I had to swallow, every double standard I was subjected to put a rock in my rucksack, to the point where it was so heavy that I could not carry it anymore.

After the assault I became more and more self-destructive in my personal life, and the more self-destructive I became, the more I excelled in my professional life. You unintentionally taught me how to compartmentalize. This made for an interesting paradox as I compensated for my self-destruction by working harder. In fact, my performance at work led to me being nominated to be the first female Corporal to instruct at the Canadian Forces School of Intelligence and Security (CFSIS), now named the Canadian Forces Military Police Academy (CFMPA).

While at the MP school, I could not get you out of my head. I was supposed to be the top MP Cpl in Canada and yet I allowed you to sexually assault me. I started to suffer from anxiety attacks and depression, and I very quickly found myself drinking to the point of passing out almost every night to try to force you out of my head so that your hatred could no longer hurt me. I let you see what I wanted you to see, and instead of disclosing your inappropriate behaviour, I wove a story to protect myself. That story went something like this: You were extremely intoxicated and tried to get with me but I pushed you away. Nothing happened between us. However, I do admit to myself that you said you could fuck the gay out of me. As I lived this narrative, I actually convinced myself that what I was telling myself was the truth, but deep down I knew the source of the scars I was carrying around.

Scars are complex. Typically, a scar is the body's natural way of healing and replacing the damaged area of skin. The scars you left me with were worse than the ones on my nose, forehead, and upper lip from diving off that thirty-foot pier into three feet of water. At least the scars on my face were nature's attempt to replace my damaged skin. The scars you left me with will never heal.

In order to never be wounded like that again and to survive the wounds you inflicted upon me, I would put on my metaphoric suit of armour. I only took it off when no one was around to see the real me. I would wait for everyone to go to bed, then I would pour a drink or two or three and tentatively remove my suit of armour, allowing the hurt and shame and disgust of myself to breathe for an hour or so. Once I cleansed my soul with my tears, I would put my suit of armour back on, go to bed, and get a couple of hours' sleep before starting all over again the next day. I kept hoping that one day I would wake up and these scars would no longer be there. Every time I feel them, they remind me of you. Do you ever think of me?

6
THE PURGE

It takes no compromise to give people their rights ... it takes no money to respect the individual. It takes no political deal to give people freedom. It takes no survey to remove repression.
— *Harvey Milk*

SOME OF THE DARKEST DAYS in our military history came when the institution decided to rid the Forces of homosexuals. In case you are not familiar with what the Purge was, let me try to explain it from my perspective. Between the 1950s and 1990s, the Canadian government forbade LGBTQ people from joining or serving in the Federal public service or the Department of National Defence. Members who ascribed to the LGBTQ community were considered mentally ill, a menace to society, and a security risk. They were cast as political subversives. They were also seen as targets for extortion by communist regimes seeking classified information. A massive hunt to eliminate these people from the ranks was carried out by the Royal Canadian Mounted Police (RCMP) for public servants and the Special Investigation Unit (SIU), a branch of the Military Police Group, for military personnel. This continued even after Pierre Elliot Trudeau's government decriminalized homosexuality in 1969. Trudeau summed up Bill C-150 in one sentence: "There's no place for the state in the bedrooms of the nation." What he didn't say was unless you are serving in our military. Essentially, he was saying that it was all right for ordinary citizens to be gay but there was no way a Canadian Forces soldier could be gay. There was no recourse for LGBTQ military members because the Canadian Charter of Rights and Freedoms did not exist until 1982. The Charter came into force on April 17, 1982. Section 15 of the Charter came into effect three years later, on April 17, 1985, to give governments time to bring their laws into line with the rights guaranteed in the section, but it still did not have any teeth for CAF members until 1992.

During this timeframe, approximately nine thousand known careers were ruined, but it is suspected that number is much greater. People were put under surveillance for months at a time, interrogated under bright lights for hours, hooked up to the "fruit machine," locked up in psychiatric wards, demoted, and dismissed with disgrace as not advantageously employable from Her Majesty's service. They lost their livelihoods and in some cases their sanity. Some escaped by taking their own lives. Those times were pure hell for all members of the LGBTQ community who chose to serve their country. I played the LGBT Purge game so well, hiding who I was at my core and pretending to be straight, that I was able to hide in plain sight and I was never subjected to the inhumane treatment from the SIU that those who came before me experienced. I escaped the "fruit machine" and I escaped any formal investigations from the SIU. Many people thought they knew I was gay, but there was just no evidence to haul me in for an interview! Do not get me wrong, this does not mean I was not hunted, because I was, but I just did not have to endure multiple hunting seasons. What I did have to go through for the entirety of my career was an underlying intolerance of me staying around despite every attempt to get rid of me. For anyone interested in what it was like to be in the military when the gays and lesbians were hunted like wild animals, you should avail yourself to filmmaker Sarah Fodey's documentary called The Fruit Machine. The CAF has just bought the rights to this film. Better late than never.

I used to consider myself one of the fortunate ones to have escaped mostly unscathed, but during the last days of my career, I finally admitted that I was covered in scars — physical and mental. Having said that, I owe a huge debt of gratitude to Michelle Douglas and Martine Roy, because like me and those who came after me, we survived by standing on their shoulders. I was able to be "out" in the later years of my career because of the hard work of some trailblazing women.

Michelle Douglas took on the Government of Canada after her discharge for being a lesbian. She started a movement that could not be stopped. In 1988, the government quietly altered the policy on homosexuality a little bit in that dismissal from the CAF was no longer automatic if you were found out. You were asked to leave, but if you chose to stay in the military and serve your country you were rewarded with no promotions, no courses, and a denial of security clearance, which was and still is required by every CAF soldier to do their job. If you consented to your release, you were released under item 5(d). A release under this item is applied to CAF members who are not advantageously employable. What a choice!

When Michelle won her case in 1992, resulting in the end of longstanding discrimination against LGBTQ members and the rescinding of Canadian Forces Administration Order (CFAO) 19-20, Homosexuality — Sexual Abnormality Investigation, Medical Examination and Disposal, which came into force in 1967, those of us still serving rejoiced. After Douglas's landmark win, all official restrictions on LGBTQ members were lifted. It did, however, take another four years for the military to recognize that same-sex couples should be entitled to the same medical benefits as their straight counterparts. A federal human rights tribunal ordered the federal government to provide the same medical, dental, and other benefits to same-sex couples, such as military housing. Other benefits included compassionate leave and leave without pay for spousal accompaniment, posting allowances, and the right to designate a gay partner for pension purposes, which took until 1999 to implement the military pension survivor benefits. Despite this movement toward normalizing homosexual service in the CAF, micro-aggressions continued to occur. Even though LGBTQ people now possessed these rights, most still did not feel free to be their authentic selves. It would take until the mid-2000s before many of us would come out of the closet and stay out without fear of rejection, reprisal, or retaliation. Until then, we hid in plain sight.

Martine Roy was one of the lead plaintiffs in the 2016 class action lawsuit that resulted in a twenty-six-million-dollar settlement being reached in 2018 for all those people affected by the Purge. Part of the Purge settlement included an apology from the Prime Minister of Canada, Justin Trudeau, as well as the eventual construction of an Ottawa national monument to memorialize those people whose careers were ruined because of their sexual orientation. I did not apply as a respondent for the LGBT Purge Class Action Settlement. I, like so many others, felt as if I did not have it half as bad as some and I did not want to take monetary funds away from others who deserved it more than me. Besides, I was not ready to admit to myself or anyone else that this had happened to me too.

    I still don't know if I am fully ready to admit my trauma, but the time has come for me to reach into the dark recesses of my heart and pull out the things I never really wanted to talk about ever again, and here I am, swallowing my pride, and doing just that.

    I am lucky in that I got to serve out a full career and some would even say achieved great success, but I guess it depends on how you define success. I pretended to be fine for thirty-five years and I would have carried on with the charade had a fellow Chief Petty Officer/Chief Warrant Officer not made the last three years of my career so difficult. Now in a position where my voice should have had the most influence, it had none because it was diminished and discounted by someone in a position of power, which was devastating. I would have thought that by the time I had reached this level of the most senior CAF non-commissioned members (NCM) that a more mature and balanced exchange of perspectives would be sought to inform decisions to make the CAF a better place to serve. I was both surprised and disappointed at the lack of inclusion and some of the Machiavellian attempts to marginalize me.

    I was forced into silence during the Purge years and never ever wanted to go back there. Yet at the pinnacle of my career, I was silenced again. This time, I was muzzled because that fellow CPO1/CWO was intimidated by me. What that person failed to understand was that diversity in our workforce does not lead to marginalized groups winning and heteronormative white men losing. It was not a zero-sum game we were playing!

Looking back over my career, I have unconsciously, and perhaps at times consciously, allowed the system to continue to operate in this exclusionary fashion. There were so many sleepless nights where I found solace at the bottom of a bottle. Unfortunately, the alcohol would wear off and I would feel worse than I did before because those initial feelings of shame and self-hatred can never be left completely behind. I used alcohol like others used the bible — it was my sanctuary, giving me momentary relief from internal pain. I found it so difficult to show emotion because that was considered a weakness, something that could be exploited. There is always that little voice in my head telling me that others, even those I love, are thinking, You are a freak! The good thing though, if there is a good thing, is that once I came out, they could no longer hurt me with their insults. I have been called a dyke too many times to count. Now, I laugh and ask if it was the big red scarlet D on my forehead or was it my beautiful wife, with her lipstick and high-heeled shoes, that gave me away!

Some of the more hurtful remarks I was subjected to came from senior NCMs, who should have known better. The worst encounter was when a male senior NCO told me that, as a gay person, "I should have been exterminated like the Jews." When I heard this my mind immediately went to the development of the Nazi persecution of the Jews. Their persecution started out as just hateful words, but soon escalated to discrimination and dehumanization, and then this atrocity concluded with the worst genocide in human history. According to this man, I was a freak of nature. Playing back his words, my mind always goes back to the Holocaust, which showed that when one group is targeted, all people are vulnerable. I was not just afraid for myself, I was afraid for all LGBTQ members in the CAF. This comment hurt me the most. It hurt me more than the sexual assault I experienced, the blatant ostracism, and even the last three years of marginalization.

Throughout my career I have flashed back to that day many times. Despite knowing in my rational mind that this bully only threatened me because he feared he was losing his power and control, I was afraid for a long time that he would carry out his threat. If Hitler could eliminate an entire race, this guy could easily get rid of me. I had never seen anyone with so much hatred in their heart. Even writing about it now, decades after the incident, I get angina pains, I start to sweat, and my mouth goes dry. This man, with his vile words, robbed me of enjoying the one thing I had wanted since I was a little girl: to serve my country with pride and distinction. I hated him because he confirmed what I had learned throughout my life, which was that I did not belong, that I was not worthy of wearing Canada's flag on my shoulder, and that I should feel ashamed to be with the person I loved.

After all the injustices I went through, the question begs to be asked: Why did I chose to stay? The answer, of course, is not that simple but one I aim to answer through this book.

7
COME OUT, COME OUT, WHOEVER YOU ARE

The single best thing about coming out of the closet is that nobody can insult you by telling you what you've just told them.
— *Rachel Maddow*

IN ONE NIGHT, my father reinforced every single shameful feeling inside me when I walked into the house after my first girlfriend dropped me off and we kissed goodnight. He was standing in the dark, lying in wait for me. He had seen it all and asked what I thought I was doing. There was no sense lying, so I gave him a smartass remark. He grabbed me by the throat, lifting my feet off the ground, and pinned me up against the wall, calling me a "fucking dyke." I was yelling, "Does it make you feel like a man? Hit me, if that will make you feel better. Go ahead and hit me." My mom finally came out of her bedroom and ordered my dad downstairs, and she told me to go to bed. The next day we did not speak of it and just went about our normal routines, which meant we walked on eggshells around each other until enough time passed and we could return to normal. This was the way we addressed problems with my father in my family — avoid, avoid, avoid at all costs talking about what happened. We trusted our mother to deal with him, and she always did because he would be on his best behaviour for awhile and then it would start all over again. It was almost like he wasn't happy unless he was tormenting one of us.

Thinking about it now, this avoidance technique would come to haunt me as a female member of the CAF, who just happened to be a lesbian. But avoidance and silence paid dividends. Keeping my mouth shut was exactly what the organization wanted from me — "Do your job but don't make waves or complain and we will reward you with on-time promotions and courses," was the silent message that was conveyed by the leadership.

Not long after the incident with my father, I finally got the courage to admit to my family that I was a lesbian. It was 1981. It was my coming out story, but the reality was that I was secretly still hiding because I still hid my authentic self in public. I remember that day like it was yesterday. I was sitting at the kitchen table, my mom facing me. I was sweating, despite it being a crisp autumn morning. I was drinking a diet coke; my mom had a coffee. I was severely hungover from a late night of drinking with friends, and my self-esteem was in the toilet. My mom was staring at me, and I finally blurted out that I am gay. She said, "I beg your pardon." More slowly and in a whisper, I repeated, "I am gay." She began to cry. I went to hug her, but she waved me off. After what seemed like an eternity, she looked up from her hands in her lap that she had been studying so intently and quietly asked what she had done wrong in raising me. My heart sunk to the pit of my stomach. How could she think she did something wrong? It was me who was the aberration. I wanted to be "different" so I would not have to lie just to be considered a normal human being and not some social deviant.

After an extremely long silence where you could have heard a pin drop, she told me she suspected but if I had not come right out and told her, then she wouldn't have known for sure and she could have continued lying to herself. She also did not want my grandmother or my aunt to find out as they would not understand. As much as my mom was embarrassed, I understood why. She was trying to protect her mother, and I got that because I would do anything to protect her. Unfortunately, I could not protect her from the knowledge that I was gay. I felt guilty that I had to put her through this.

Sitting at the kitchen table, I learned the true meaning of self-loathing. I also learned that even if everyone in my immediate family accepted me, there might still be some relatives who would not, and

I had never considered that. My mom was asking me to hide who I was so as not to make anyone uncomfortable and to maintain family unity. This taught me that even those who love you can be ashamed of you. It also taught me to conceal my identity and pretend to be someone I was not.

As a very astute friend told me, my mother was my hero. When I came out to her, the hurt and disappointment in her eyes was gut wrenching. However, she still loved me and by default accepted who I was. Instinctively, I knew that for everyone else out there, their feelings toward me could and would be exponentially negative. I became highly adept at sensing danger, and like a clever octopus, I became a master at camouflage.

Coming out to family did not mean you were free to come out outside the safe confines of your home. Society at that time was still very aggressive toward the LGBTQ community. Even though it was 1981 when I had that conversation with my mother at her kitchen table, I chose not to truly live openly until the mid-2000s for fear of retribution, whether that was in the form of physical violence or career restrictions. The era I grew up in and my mother's request to hide who I really was influenced my decision to never show affection to my partner in public. Even to this day, I do not feel comfortable holding my wife's hand in public or kissing her at the airport when I came back from a six-month deployment. Thankfully, my wife understands and does not have an issue with this. She recognizes the path I had to walk. Our children don't understand though and think that we are crazy. I tried to explain to them that I did not want to be the topic of conversation at someone's dinner table when their small child asked why two women were holding hands. My one daughter replied by saying that should be the mother's choice to answer not yours. Of course, our children are a product of their generation just as I was. But then my wife stepped in to help me, as she always does. She defended our decision by saying that it makes the times we do sneak a kiss or a pat on the bum in public when no one is looking more special.

In the military in the eighties and nineties, you had a coming out story forced upon you every time you were posted from one location to another. You had to include all your personal information on the unit's nominal roll, which everyone in the unit had access to. If that was not bad enough, nine times out of ten the gaining unit had a welcoming reception for all newly posted in personnel and their families. Back then it was extremely stressful to get posted from one place to the next because your private life would become public knowledge to a whole new group of people, and for a period of time, you became the talk of the town. I hated being posted.

At these welcoming parties the Commanding Officer (CO) would normally introduce you and your family to the rest of the unit during a section barbeque. I recall one particular barbeque where the CO introduced my wife and I. Out of nowhere a junior non-commissioned member loudly proclaimed that there was no way he was working for any split-ass dyke. The sad part was not that he said it out loud but the fact that no senior personnel corrected him. I have to assume they heard him because I heard him and I was on the opposite side of the room, and all the senior NCOs were at the same table as me. After the CO was done speaking, I excused myself and walked right over to his table, where he was sitting with a bunch of other junior members and his wife. All I kept thinking as I walked across the floor, with all eyes on me, was don't let them see you sweat. I pulled up a chair and sat beside him, and with a smile on my face, told him that I would be specifically asking the chain of command to have him on my shift. I then proceeded to ask him if he had children. He went quiet. Apparently, he wasn't so brave when the target of his hatred confronted him. His wife answered for him. I directed my attention to her as she replied, "We have two children, a boy and a girl." I asked her how she would like it if her daughter came home and told her that one little girl in her class said that the other kids were being mean and refused to play with her on the playground. I could see her visibly swallow as she took a minute before responding that she would not like it.

I kept my word and asked for him on my shift. The leadership complied with my request because he apparently had a bad reputation for amassing public complaints against him. Despite having white male privilege, he was a little like me — a social outcast. Once we had an opportunity to work together for a period, I quickly realized that he had complaints against him because he did his job, and on this wing, people were not used to that. The more I supported him the more I could see small changes in him. The number of public complaints went down, he would open up and ask more questions, and his biggest transformation: he asked me to be his mentor. He turned out to be one of the best patrolmen I have ever met, and he did not want to work on any other shift but mine. He was simply misunderstood, and when not pre-judged, he excelled at his job. He was able to put his bigotry aside and see me as just another human being.

Coming out is always a personal story and can bring great relief and joy or can be fraught with great sadness and fear. Some of my relationships where I had to come out were joyful and some not so much.

My first lesbian relationship was with a woman ten years my senior who I met on the baseball diamond. She and I lived together for an entire year while I finished high school. When I returned to my parents' home to go to college, things between us started to fall apart. By first semester we had broken up. My next relationship was with Tracy, who I had fallen very hard for. We met on the ball diamond. She played for the military team in Trenton, while I played for a civilian team as I was not yet in the military. The year was 1983. Not long after we started dating, I moved in with her. I did not even really know who she was, but anything was better than living under my father's roof. I could not watch him make everyone around him miserable. I found out shortly after I started seeing Tracy that she was still seeing her ex-girlfriend, who lived in Germany. This should not have come as a surprise to me because she left that woman for me.

When I met her, she had just taken a three-year hiatus from her military occupation to act as a flight attendant on military aircraft. As the military flew to Germany on a regular basis, Tracy always volunteered for these flights. I stupidly overlooked this because deep down I felt I was not worthy of someone loving me. I even overlooked the time that she verbally attacked my sister in my parents' house. Tracy and my sister despised each other. My sister has always been a good judge of character and she could sense that this woman did not have a good heart. As it was told to me, my sister was downstairs, and while I was passed out upstairs, Tracy took advantage of that time and started spewing personal attacks against my sister. When my sister would not bite, Tracy started to say very mean things about my mother, knowing that this would get under my sister's skin and that she would react, which she did. Tracy kept hurling insults about my mother until my father came out of his bedroom and told her to get out of his house.

After getting kicked out of my parents' house, Tracy came upstairs and woke me up and told me we were leaving. Not knowing what had gone on because I was passed out drunk upstairs and did not hear any of the commotion, I stupidly followed, and we left. The next day I asked Tracy what happened, and she told me that my sister started insulting her for no reason, so she reacted and fought back. I believed her because I knew they did not get along. What she failed to tell me was that my father kicked her out of the house and that the reason my sister was attacking her was because she was insulting my mother. A week later my mom and my aunt, who was visiting, came to my work and said they wanted to take me to lunch. This was when I learned the truth about what happened that evening. My mother had overheard all the insults directed at her. She laid silently in bed, crying. She was hurt because she had been nothing but nice to Tracy. She had opened her home to her despite not really accepting the homosexual way of life. I was devastated but I went back to Tracy, turning my back on my family.

I did a lot of stupid stuff because of this woman. For example, a few months later Tracy and I headed to her brother's wedding in

Saskatoon, except we did not fly commercial air, we flew "military service air." Normally, this would not be worth telling except civilians were not permitted on these flights. We concluded that it would be a great idea if I borrowed one of our friend's military uniforms and pretended to be her. I did look enough like her that minor scrutiny of her National Defence Identification 20 card would pass. While I got away with it, there were some close calls. Not recognizing the severity of what I had done, I thought it was funny — a story to be told at cocktail parties with our friends. That was until I learned what stolen valour meant. I realized the depth of my transgression and felt ashamed. I would not feel this way again about stolen valour until near the end of my career.

The year 1987 was a monumental one for Tracy and I. Tracy received a promotion to the rank of Warrant Officer (WO) and a posting message. She was moving to Chilliwack, BC, and I went with her. This caused a huge divide between me and my mom that took several years to heal. She had never forgiven Tracy for the New Year's Eve incident. Nor did she forgive me for choosing Tracy over her. I was in Chilliwack for less than three months when I received the message from the CAF to go to Vancouver's Canadian Forces Recruiting Centre (CFRC) to swear my oath of allegiance to the Queen. On November 12, 1987, I embarked upon a military flight, on my way to Cornwallis. I left with a partner and returned a single person, and my mom could not have been happier.

After recruit graduation in Cornwallis in February 1988, I went to Saint-Jean-sur-Richelieu to take six months of French language training. While playing baseball in the summer of 1988, I met Janie. I thought I needed someone to help me ward off the demons I lived with every day, and I convinced myself that Janie could be that special someone. In February 1989, one full year after graduating from recruit training in Cornwallis, language school in Saint-Jean, and my basic MP course at CFB Borden, I headed off to my first posting in Saint-Jean as a qualified MP. I had a badge and a gun and I was ready to police the CAF. I was the only person on my entire course that asked for and received a French base as their posting choice. I was going back to what was familiar and comfortable. Unfortunately, after six months of speaking only English on my trades training course, I had lost all the French I had learned when I was posted there in 1988.

    So why go back? It is the typical idiomatic expression: girl meets girl. I was going back for Janie. I was certain she was the one. I fell in love with her during baseball season in 1988. I did not give two thoughts about how I was going to do my job, not being able to speak the language. My financial situation (I was a Private), forced me to live in Military Barracks. I was housed at the Megaplex, in the Blue Section, on the fifth floor, and had two roommates in my family unit. Francine and Janie were to be my new roommates. Francine was a Warrant Officer (WO) who was a resource management clerk, and Janie was, at that time, a Sergeant (Sgt) who was a supply technician but was being employed outside her occupation as an instructor at recruit school. At that time, Saint-Jean was the location of all French-speaking training for the École de leadership et de recrues des Forces canadiennes. How fortuitous that I would be living in the same family unit as Janie since I had asked for this posting because of her!

    It did not take long before Janie and I connected, and we soon moved out into our own apartment. Janie was an amazing woman, and I did not deserve her. For two years, things between us were fantastic. We both fell head over heels in love with each other, despite our little ups and downs while we adjusted to each other. Of course, I didn't tell her about my formative years. I didn't want her to run away, so I let her meet my father without any prejudgments from me. She was such a wonderful woman that it was really quite easy for me to hide all my ugly warts for the first two years while I was learning to love her. Janie was not a big drinker, so I cut way back on my drinking except for when she would go to the field overnight with the recruits or go home to her parents' house.

    If I wanted to drink and she was in town, I would do it on my last night shift so that she would be at work before I came home. She knew that if I wasn't home shortly after 6:00 a.m. then I mostly likely had a case that I was investigating, so it didn't surprise her when I wasn't home that morning. What did surprise her was finding me half hanging out of the car, passed out drunk, when she came down to get in her car to go to the office. She woke me and told me to get upstairs. What she did not know was that I got into this state because earlier that evening I met you at the local neighbourhood bar and you decided that I did not deserve your respect as a human being. When I refused to tell her why she found me in that state, our relationship started to go downhill from there. I became emotionally inaccessible, and my drinking got even more out of control. I was now too wounded to care about hiding my drinking from her. Now, I was drinking all the time, not just on my set of days off. She spent most of her weekends at her parents' home, approximately three hours from our apartment.

Once I started drinking, I would not stop until I reached the bottom of the bottle, and the more accomplished I got at drinking, the more alcohol it took to achieve that high. At my peak I could consume half to three-quarters of a bottle of rye in one sitting, but with that came blackouts, which were quite frequent. I was also a mean drunk and would look for any excuse to pick a fight with Janie. I never fought when I was sober, but rather would use passive-aggressive communication to deceptively manipulate and control a situation. For some stupid reason, I believed that our situation would be worse if Janie knew the real reason why I was passed out drunk, half hanging out of my car.

She needed to get away from me, for her own sanity. Unfortunately, I was not strong enough to let her go first. I didn't want to hurt her but I could not help myself. Janie's saving grace came in 1993, when we were both posted. She was getting away from me. Janie was heading to Valcartier, Quebec, and I was returning to Borden, Ontario. Nothing was the same for us after that fateful night after work in the neighbourhood bar. I could no longer be intimate with her. I would sink into depressions, and communication became minimal and was often negative after a brief period of being together.

Instead of accepting our differences, I criticized them. The fact that I could not be honest with her about that night resulted in our demise.

After Janie left, I found myself thinking more and more about Tracy. I thought about her a lot when Janie and I got together, but those thoughts faded somewhat in our first year together. When Tracy left me, it was very painful and difficult, and it was a time of great loneliness, confusion, and insecurity. Despite everything that had happened between us, I still begged Tracy to take me back. I lost every ounce of pride I ever had. When she refused, I plunged into a pity party, and I found myself wanting to seek validation through a new relationship. Unfortunately, it was at the expense of Janie. What I did not realize when I originally started pursuing this amazing woman was that I was on the rebound from Tracy. I was suffering from real and imagined abandonment issues, and thoughts of inadequacy and inferiority were always at the forefront of my psyche. Regardless of what happened to me in the bar that night, and having internalized these feelings, a long-term relationship with Janie wasn't going to happen, because no matter how well she treated me, how much she loved me, I sabotaged whatever love we shared. Another relationship ended because of my behaviour and insecurities.

Next up was CFB Borden. The year was 1993, and as the first two Corporals posted to CFSIS, Cpl Marc Picard and I had to rewrite the entire basic entry level course lesson plans to match the qualification standard that was decided before we arrived at the school. We put our heads down and worked extremely hard to get this done before Marc's course would start in the spring of 1994. Then, after all that, I had to translate all the English lesson plans into French so my course would have the same standard of training as the English class. As close as Marc and I were, even he didn't know I was a functioning alcoholic because I hid it — or at least I thought he didn't know. To say that it was a long winter was an understatement, especially since I was left to figure out how to handle the trauma of that sexual assault. So when spring came, I could not get to the Accommodations building fast enough. That was where we had to sign up to join the Military Women's Softball team.

I was rushing into the building because I had a badminton date at the gym with my Officer Commanding (OC). I was not paying attention and almost ran into a senior NCO. I looked up and who was standing there but Tracy. I almost shit my pants, and in fact, I looked like I saw a ghost. To make matters worse, she was the baseball coach as well. In true Tracy fashion, she benched me the first exhibition game we played just to show me she still had control over me.

Later that spring, we were practising when a woman came walking across the baseball diamond, and I instantly fell in love. I asked another lady on the infield with me who that the woman was, and she replied, "Back off, Nicki, she's straight." I tried to stay away but I just knew that this was the woman I wanted to spend the rest of my life with. Judi and I quickly became fast friends. After spending a lot of time together, I finally asked her, "If you know we are all gay, why do you keep hanging around with us?" Judi had two children and a husband. Judi stunned me by replying, "What makes you think I am what you think I am?"

I jumped back like I had been burned by a hot pan when Judi alluded to the fact that I might have a chance with her. My response was to run away, and I stayed away for two weeks, but every minute of every waking moment of those two weeks I thought of her. I didn't want to give in to these feelings because I knew I was not worthy of this woman. I did not want to hurt her, like I had done to Janie. I knew the person I wanted to be but I was afraid I could not change. I was afraid to let out the secrets I had been holding in since my early teens, because I was fairly certain, if she knew, she wouldn't even want to be friends, let alone lovers. All that being said, I just could not stay away.

After spending four years at the Canadian Forces School of Intelligence and Security, having fulfilled multiple positions, I was transferred to the MP Guardhouse, just up the hill from the school. I had arrived at the school as a Corporal and left as a Sergeant, without really having been in a leadership position. I watched how others led, to get an idea of how to deal with subordinates, and it was very transactional in nature. Since I wanted to be like them and advance like them, I assumed this style of leadership as well. I was in charge of the Investigations Section and essentially fired almost every person they put in there with me. I would fire them because they could not keep up with me. I thought everyone should work like I did, putting work first against all else. I would think of them as lazy if they did not have as many investigations on their plate as I did. I would holler and scream at them and belittle them if I had to rewrite their reports to meet my exacting standards. In other words, I was a tyrant.

A lot of people wanted to come to the Investigations Section because it was straight day work as opposed to shift work, but most would prefer to work shift work than work with me. Once when I tried to fire someone, and I went to the Police Operations Warrant Officer to do so, he told me he had no one else to replace them, as I had fired them all. He then looked at me and said, "Did you ever consider that it might not be them?" I thought about that comment for a long time and got a little better when I went to Cold Lake, but I was still a very transactional leader. I did not understand why it worked for the men but not for me.

8
My Eventual Saviour

At any given moment, you have the power to say: this is not how the story is going to end.
— *Christine Mason Miller*

ON SEPTEMBER 5, 1994, I gave in to my desires and called Judi at home and asked if she wanted to meet me at the Rod and Gun, a local drinking establishment for military members. We began dating, and everyone had something to say about it, including my mother. Some of our so-called friends made statements like Judi was just hunting for a pension and I just wanted to play house for awhile. Someone even had the gall to tell my mother that Judi was just after my pension. My mom told me that Judi was not welcome in her home. My mom was dead set against me dating anyone with children. She believed that the children did not ask or consent to be in that type of family dynamic and it was not fair to the children to expose them to ridicule from their friends. Just as I was a product of my generation, she too was a product of hers.

I made the choice to not visit my mom and dad in Trenton until Judi was welcome. It was one of the hardest choices I had to make, considering we were only about two hours away from each other, and I used to come home almost twice a month from Borden before Judi and I became involved. I did, however, speak to my mom almost daily on the telephone. We could be on the phone with each other for hours and not really talk about anything but simply enjoy the sound of each other's voice. Luckily, my sister and her husband and child were coming to Trenton to visit from British Columbia, and they were landing in Toronto. My mom called me and asked if I would pick them up from the airport because Judi had a minivan and my sister and her family had more luggage than would fit in my parents' car. I agreed to go and pick them up on the condition that Judi be allowed to come with me. My mom agreed, and they met for the first time approximately four months after we started dating. That year, the federal human rights tribunal ordered the military to provide same-sex benefits to military members, which included the right to declare common-law status. Once you swore an affidavit, you were then entitled to the same benefits as a heterosexual member with a spouse and children. I met with my Officer Commanding (OC), and in an affidavit swore to the OC that I had lived with Judi for a continuous period of at least one year in a lesbian relationship and that I represented Judi as my life partner.

My OC was also my badminton partner. We both loved badminton and played often as partners during lunch hour. We also competed together at the CAF national level. We were highly competitive, and I recall one time during CAF Nationals when we were playing doubles and both of us were playing terribly. We were losing badly. I happened to be in the back court when our opponents made a shot that I should have been able to return. I committed an unforced error, and in anger I picked up the birdie and smashed it at the very same time that my OC turned around. It hit her square in the mouth. She was very mad! I could not help it — I burst out laughing. That moment changed our momentum, and we ended up winning the game and set.

Naturally, we had undressed in front of each other to take our showers after sports, so it was particularly shameful for me when I had to tell her that I was a lesbian. I felt the fear of rejection and ostracization for being forced by law to hide who I was. I also had flashbacks to my teenage years playing hockey when I walked into the dressing room and overheard my friend and some other girls on my hockey team calling me creepy. I was so nervous I could barely hold down any food for a week before I had to go into her office and make my declaration. I thought she would feel betrayed because of the many misleading statements and outright lies I had told her to adhere to the rules I was required to follow. I garnered the courage and told her the truth. She never batted an eye and simply signed my declaration of common-law status with Judi, who eventually would become my lawfully wedded wife in 2012. She was truly happy for us and later told me that she knew that we were together, because according to her "you could not hide a love that strong." That was the last time that I worked with this woman, and yet on June 15, 2022, she came all the way from New York, where she was living with her husband, to say goodbye to me as I retired from the CAF.

Coming out to my OC and declaring common-law status with Judi did not mean that the closet door burst open and I came rushing out. Rather, it was like opening the door a tiny crack to peek out and then slamming it shut again, before the negative attitudes toward me could cause me further harm from a career perspective and from a psychological perspective.

Our first couple of years together were very rocky. I drank on all my days off, and Judi was too scared of my temper to say anything to me. I had developed a bad habit of not sleeping at night. I would go to bed but sleep would evade me, so I would eventually get up and wander the halls of the little house we lived in. On average I would get about two to three hours of sleep a night unless I was drunk, and then I would pass out.

Unlike any of my other relationships, Judi made me feel I was worthy. She made me want to become that person I could see in my mind's eye. She made me want to be someone a partner could count on, someone a child could look up to, someone a mother could be proud of. I kept trying to get there, but every time I would start to get close, something would scare me off; I would revert to my old coping mechanisms, which for the most part included avoidance and drinking myself into oblivion.

I would sober up and promise myself never to do it again, only to repeat the same pattern over and over again. I tried everything to drive her away so she could not hurt me, but she saw through that and held on for the ride of her life. Why she and the girls stayed with me, I still don't know, but I am grateful they did because I think I would have drunk myself to death if had they disappeared out of my life like everyone else.

Even though I had been excelling professionally before her, it was after we started dating that I began to buckle down. I started to top every career course I went on and develop a reputation as the fixer. I would be chosen to go into a unit to fix morale or production or any other issue that unit was suffering from. I loved this role because I did not want to be overlooked. I wanted to excel at the same rate as my peers, and for the most part I did. I excelled up until I reached the rank of Chief Warrant Officer, which is where my career management and progression changed from being controlled by my occupation (Military Police) to being controlled by the environmental Command I belonged to (Royal Canadian Air Force).

It took my mother a long time to trust Judi. She saw what the breakup with Tracy and Janie did to my heart, and she wanted to make sure, especially with children now involved in the relationship, that we were both serious about making this relationship work. In fact, it wasn't until I deployed to Bosnia that their relationship turned a corner. As a mother herself, Judi understood the feelings my mom would be experiencing having her youngest child deployed to a conflict zone. Twice a week I would call home, and Judi would immediately call my mom after we spoke to tell her how I was doing. She also gave up some of her time so I could call my mother and speak with her. I never asked her to do this, she simply volunteered, knowing I would want to hear my mom's voice and that my mom would want to know I was okay. My mother and Judi built an unbreakable bond after that deployment.

In 2000 our family finally left Borden and we were off to Cold Lake, Alberta. The trip from Ontario to Alberta was long, given that one of our girls was a tween and the other a precocious ten-year-old. We drove a little Saturn with no air conditioning. In addition to the four of us in the car, there were our two cats, Floozie and Bella. We tried to make the most of the trip by creating holiday dollars and asking the girls geography and history questions at every major city. Whenever they got an answer right, they would get holiday dollars that they could cash in at each stop or save them and cash them in at the end of the trip for real money. It must have left a good impression on the girls because both spoke fondly of it during my retirement departure with dignity (DWD) ceremony.

During that same trip across Canada, my career manager had called and asked if I wanted to deploy to Ethiopia. I explained that I would love to, but I was halfway across the country, making our way to our next posting, so the answer would be no. My career manager said no problem and that he would be deploying me on the next rotation that came up. While I didn't expect his call to come two days after we arrived in Cold Lake, it did, and I was ready. I deployed to Bosnia in January 2001. I spent August to December 2000 conducting pre-deployment training in Petawawa, Ontario.

I returned home in early December and began preparing ready-made meals for Judi and the girls. As I was the cook in the family, I didn't want my girls to starve to death. I filled our freezer with all sorts of meals packaged separately for all of them. Every meal would have a protein, a starch, and a vegetable. The freezer was packed, and they had enough to get them through the four-and-a-half-month timeframe. Judi worked until 5:00 p.m., so the girls were responsible for making a fresh salad so that dinner could be ready before 6:00 p.m., and homework and prep for the next day could be completed before the children's bedtime. For the most part it ran like clockwork until they ran out of ready-made dinners. Then, according to our youngest daughter, who was ten years old at the time, they were no strangers to the food court!

9
Deployments — Bosnia, Jakarta, Cyprus, and the Return Home

There is no hunting like the hunting of man, and those who have hunted armed men long enough and liked it, never care for anything else thereafter.
— **Ernest Hemingway**

HATE KNOWS NO BOUNDS and it will seep into any crack if permitted. Despite certain official homosexual documents being repealed, homophobia was still running rampant in the 1990s and even into the early 2000s, especially when you had to deploy or went on a tasking or even a course. Being away from home on a deployment or a course rendered homosexuals more vulnerable. Deployment screenings and working in close proximity with your peers on course or on deployment made it more difficult to hide and you had to be on your guard 24/7.

We had been in Borden for seven years when I was suddenly posted and was told to choose where I wanted to go. I chose Cold Lake, and it felt as if no sooner did I arrive than I was getting off a military aircraft in Bosnia — a Muslim country where gay people were persecuted for their sin and ethnic cleansing of the civilian population was commonplace between the Bosnian Serbs, the Bosnian Muslims, and the Croatians in order to better establish their land claims associated with their sought-after independence. Obviously, I could not reveal that I was gay, or I could be persecuted for this crime while in Bosnia, nor could I reveal my secret to OSCAR Company (COY) Officer Commanding (OC) and the Company Sergeant-Major (CSM) as I might not have been able to deploy. It was extremely difficult to lie to these guys, considering they were the ones who had my back on the battlefield. I needed to establish my value to them almost immediately because MP who had never deployed were considered a nuisance. It was believed that we brought nothing to the fight because we could only police our own soldiers.

Moreover, as a MP, if you had served overseas at a Mission Security Unit you were making more Foreign Service pay than an Infantry soldier who had deployed to conflict zones on multiple occasions. I managed to establish trust with the CSM and the OC, which permeated down to the troops. They treated me like I was one of their own. I was not used to this type of treatment, especially from men who I interacted with daily. In fact, the OC loved to tease. When he saw me peeing on the side of the road one day, he pulled up beside my jeep, and I was in such a hurry to pull up my combat pants that I ended up peeing on my handgun. He just laughed and had his driver carry on. When I got back to the camp the Private on guard duty stopped me going into the gate and handed me a roll of toilet paper and told me that the OC said it was a one-for-one exchange. Everyone got a big laugh out of this. We had a lot of fun, and I got very close with the OC and finally told him the truth. He didn't blink an eye. He asked if I was intentionally keeping this a secret from the Company, and I told him that I was. He wanted to know if anyone had been teasing or harassing me about being a homosexual. He told me if they did to tell him as he would deal with them. I was not used to being treated so well. He and I remained very close for the remainder of the tour and used to have some great discussions about the military justice system and our ethos.

I felt extremely lucky to be with OSCAR COY because my OC and CSM took me everywhere with them. When they were conducting a raid, my OC and I were brought along to conduct traffic control and guard seized weapons. All the other MP attached to the different Companies were left to sit in their bunks as their OCs did not include them in anything that the soldiers were doing. OSCAR COY was the lead company to conduct an operation, and the MP Detachment Commander wanted to put a senior Sgt in charge of the

MP response. My OC would hear none of that and told the MP OC that his MP Sgt would be in charge, and he didn't care that the other MP Sgt was senior to me, he trusted me. The MP OC conceded, and I ran the MP response while my OC ran the Infantry response. The mission was a huge success. Near the end of the tour, as we were getting our Theatre Personnel Evaluation Reports (PER) the OC wanted me to call him while I signed my MP PER. He wanted to know what my scores were and basically said if I wasn't completely right dressed there was going to be an issue. He need not have worried.

When I returned from deployment, after being in and out of our household for the past nine months, I had some time off to reacquaint myself with my family. It was not easy, as everything in our household had changed. Now, Judi was doing everything, and I felt like a stranger who needed to ask where the coffee cups were because she re-arranged the cupboards one night when she was feeling particularly lonely and missing me. I don't know about others, but it took a long time for me to adjust to her new routine. Truth be told, it was also a blow to my ego, that she and the kids had adjusted just fine while I was gone. Judi had established a whole network of friends who I had never met. The girls had a school routine that I needed to learn. For the first couple of weeks, I actually felt like a guest in my own home. I was even asking if I could have something to eat.

By this time, I had started to feel that things were not quite right with me, but I didn't know exactly what was wrong. I would cry at the drop of a hat when I had never cried before that. Every time I thought about our Bosnian family that we adopted while we were there, I would break out in tears. I had not drank in six months, and should have stayed dry but did not. It was the first time since I was thirteen or fourteen that I went more than a week without having something to drink. Unfortunately, the pressures at work and at home were my catalyst.

I also knew there was something seriously wrong with my emotional wellbeing when I was looking in the freezer one night after supper and I asked Judi where the ham in the freezer came from. She replied,

"Easter." I repeated my question and she again responded, "Easter." I said, "No, where did it come from?" She raised her voice and shouted that it came from my mother, who brought it for Easter. I started to cry. She said "what is wrong with you" as she laughed! I stopped crying and never cried again in front of her for a very, very long time.

Just as I was getting comfortable in the home, it was time to go back to work. I was put in charge of the Investigations Cell. I was asked to pick my staff, so I did. However, the Unit CWO was not happy with my pick of investigators and told me he was putting a certain individual in the office with me. I did not want this person, as if I did, I would have picked them. I was told they were a great investigator and would be a perfect addition to the team. I finally conceded. It was at this moment that I saw the Unit CWO's true colours. He told me that if the Cpl, who he forced on me, did not agree to use all their annual leave as a day worker, then they could not have the job as investigator. Investigators only work from 0800 hrs to 1630 hrs, Monday to Friday, unless they are the duty investigator. When you are a day worker your annual leave is one for one, meaning if you take five days off, it is just five days. If you are a shift worker and want five days off, it costs you five days to get twenty days off. This is because when you are on shift you are on shift for five straight twelve-hour days, and you need five days without shifts to transition to the other twelve-hour cycle. In essence, time off as a shift worker is highly more advantageous than a day worker.

I could not believe what I was hearing! I confronted the Unit CWO and asked what kind of vindictive game he was playing. I warned off the Cpl despite me not even wanting them in the beginning, but I knew this was the right thing to do because this Cpl really wanted to be an investigator.

This was not the only time this CWO did something I did not agree with. For instance, we were sitting in merit boards, and we had our top five Cpls already chosen when he walked in and turned the list upside down. All the other heads of departments agreed to change the order of the ranking but me. I was appalled that the old boys network was being played out in front of me, with no attempt to hide it. I asked to speak with the Unit CWO and went into his office and told him I disagreed with what he did and that I would never do something so vindictive. He responded by saying, "If you ever get to my rank —" But I cut him off, replying, "It is not if I get to your rank, it is when I get there. And when I get there, I will never abuse my leadership power like you just did." With that, he told me to get up and stand to attention when I addressed him. I replied, "Oh, we're going to play this stupid game, are we?" I rose from my chair and stood to attention. He kicked me out of his office. Despite being insubordinate, he never charged me. I think it was because he did not know how.

Jakarta and Returning to Canada (2003–2007)

Judi had been bugging me for years to ask for a posting abroad, and I always put her off saying, as lesbians, we would not be accepted. She continued to bring it up in conversation, so eventually I asked the career manager, and you know the adage, be careful what you ask for because you just might get it? Well, I got it!

I was playing hockey in Borden when I received a call from the career manager asking me if I would like to go to Jakarta. I said sure, but then he reminded me that Judi should have a say as well. So, after the game, I quickly undressed and called Judi at work back in Cold Lake. At first, she thought that something was wrong because I never called her at work unless it was an emergency. Once we established that I was okay and that I did not get hurt playing hockey, I asked Judi if she wanted to be posted to the embassy in Jakarta.

She said, "Certainly, but where is Jakarta?"

"I don't know, I forgot to ask."

"Hold on a minute, I'll go get the atlas." She wasn't long coming back to the phone, and in a very excited voice told me to tell the career manager yes. Her decision was based on the fact that it is six degrees off the equator.

That was how naive we were. Little did we know that Indonesia had the largest Muslim population in the world and that homosexuality was against the law. Before saying yes, I remember asking the career manager if he knew that I was gay and that my spouse is a woman, and he said he knew. So, I asked, "Then, if you know, why are you sending us to Jakarta where homosexuality is against the law?" He replied, "Don't worry about it, you'll be okay!"

So off we went for a four-year secondment to a Canadian Embassy with Global Affairs Canada, but we almost didn't get to go because the Indonesian government was refusing to give Judi a diplomatic passport and I was insistent that she have one. Indonesia didn't know what to call Judi because they don't recognize same sex couples. The Canadian government sent the Indonesian government a giant fruit basket and suggested that she be called the HOH, head of household. They agreed, and Judi was able to secure a diplomatic passport and accompany the girls and me. Even the dog got a passport before Judi.

Things were good, for the most part. Judi and the children enjoyed the posting as much as I did. Having never felt safe in my entire career, going to the largest Muslim population in the world turned out to be a blessing in disguise. Here, I was accepted, even by the Muslims whose religion forbade my kind. All Canadian diplomatic staff were phenomenal and accepted our family as one of their own. I never had to hide. It was tough leaving a place where you enjoyed going to work every day and nobody put you down, harassed you, or stole your ideas. It is so weird to say, but the only time in my career that I could be my authentic self was in a country where homosexuality was actually against the law.

The girls went to the Jakarta International High School and Middle School, but both were located on the same campus. Judi immediately took on the role of the community coordinator and would help incoming embassy staff and their families transition to this location. She was also responsible for planning monthly social events for the staff and their families, which included the Summer Olympics, Jakarta Style, The Amazing Race, Climbing Mount Merapi, Horseback Riding, and all sorts of pot luck parties.

Our tour in Indonesia was a roller coaster of multiple significant incidents peppered throughout our stay there. In the first two weeks I was there, radicals bombed the Marriott Hotel, and I was the only Canadian in the embassy, left to manage and direct the locally engaged staff (LES) and ensure the ambassador could make it back to the embassy safely. Welcome to Jakarta, WO Belanger! Another time, Judi had been shopping at the Australian embassy twenty-four hours to the minute before the embassy was bombed.

A year after we got there, on December 26, 2004, an undersea earthquake with a magnitude of 9.1 struck off the northern coast of the Indonesian island of Sumatra, resulting in a tsunami hitting most of southeast Asia. The tsunami killed at least 225,000 people across a dozen countries, with Indonesia, Sri Lanka, India, Maldives, and Thailand sustaining the most damage. The coastline of Indonesia's Aceh province was devastated by the tsunami, including Banda Aceh, the closest major city, which is where we established Canada House to help clean up and rebuild the damage caused to that province's infrastructure.

Next came the avian influenza H1N1 scare, followed by the second Bali bombing, and then Mount Merapi spewed lava everywhere. And finally, before our four years were up, we had the great flood of Jakarta. I waded through chest-high dirty sewer water to ensure all the Canadian-based residents of Executive Paradiso, the housing complex where we lived, were okay. Our oldest daughter was told to go check on a Canadian diplomat who lived down the street because her husband was in Canada visiting. Being smart, like kids are, she decided to walk on the sawhorses that the local men sit on when they aren't working. She thought she could jump from sawhorse to sawhorse without ever getting wet. She didn't think it through though because the seats of the sawhorses were not nailed down. The scream that came out of her mouth when the first sawhorse she jumped on tipped up and all the cockroaches that were hiding underneath it fell off onto her body and into her hair was loud enough to be heard throughout the gated complex. I also had to arrange to get our people out of the complex in rubber zodiac boats, and there was nothing funnier than seeing the Canadian Defence Attaché's Assistant standing up in a zodiac in his Navy white uniform, trying to get to the airport. I was so disappointed I didn't have a camera on me. The flood was the last major incident to occur before we returned to Canada in 2007.

About twelve months after arriving on post in Jakarta, I had to return to Canada to attend my leadership course in Saint-Jean. Again, misogyny and bigotry would rear its ugly head. Some of the men on course, who would soon be promoted to Warrant Officer (WO), if they were not already wearing the rank in an acting capacity, would pretend to cough and say dyke while putting their hands over their mouths. Sadly, this did not shock me, even considering the type of course we were on. These same gentlemen thought they were extremely funny when one of them asked if he could tell a joke to the class. The instructor agreed and his joke was: "What do lawyers and lesbians have in common? They both don't do dick." The joke was not so bad and even I laughed to cover up my how uncomfortable I was because no one, not even the institute's Regimental Sergeant-Major (RSM), corrected this man. Messages like this made me feel the need to stay in the closet to maintain my secrecy. I had to be on constant alert not to reveal my authentic self, whether wittingly or unwittingly, which caused vast amounts of stress. The contrast in culture between the Canadians in Jakarta and those in the military in Canada was a stark reminder of what awaited me upon my permanent return to Canada. After spending three weeks on course, I was happy to get back to Jakarta.

Despite all the initial misgivings, we thoroughly enjoyed that posting as a family, and I professionally thrived in this environment. All my misgivings were for not because although I was scared to go to a Muslim country where homosexuality was against the law, this was the one place where I could be my authentic self. Embassy staff, both Canadian diplomats and LES, accepted us with open arms. It was here where I really learned to be the leader I was for the remainder of my career. I watched as members of the embassy made sure that other people's highest priority needs were being met. Across the spectrum of leadership styles, I had never seen this style of leadership before but instinctively knew this was who I was at my very core.

While mentally I had discovered my leadership groove, physically, I was starting to have significant health issues. Soon after arriving in Jakarta, my feet were constantly falling asleep while doing any sort of physical activity and my legs felt like they had twenty-pound weights attached to the ankles. I thought maybe my running shoes needed to be replaced, that I wore them out, so I got new ones. When that didn't fix the problem, I blamed it on the heat. We used to play squash in 110-degree heat in an enclosed room for hours. I stopped playing for awhile, but my legs continued to cramp up and my feet continued to fall asleep when walking. Since there was no doctor for us in Jakarta, I waited until I got back to Canada to have this condition looked at.

We brought my parents over every year that we were there, usually in early December, and they would stay until February. It was phenomenal to be able to share this with them, especially my mom, whose dream was to walk across the Bridge over the River Kwai, which we did one year. When visiting Vietnam, we stayed in the hotel that housed the American officers during the war, climbed Marble Mountain, and visited China Beach and the War Remnants Museum. I think the highlight for both my mom and dad was having high tea with the ambassador in his residence. They even received official gold-embossed invitations.

Leaving Jakarta was difficult as we had developed some very close relationships, especially with our maid and house manager, Lestari. I did however insist that she and my driver be hired by my replacement. It was my unofficial responsibility to make sure they had employment after I departed. Both her and the driver had it made as my replacement was single and lived in an apartment. Unfortunately, we could not find a placement for our gardener, despite our best efforts.

Lestari was so funny. I was not allowed in the kitchen because I was the "big boss," so if I went in, she would ask me what I wanted and shoo me out at the same time. Her and Judi had a very special relationship because Lestari was empowered by Judi. I remember the Indonesian movers coming to the house to pack up all our stuff to get ready to go back to Canada. Lestari, Judi, and I were all standing there, watching these men write Mr. Belanger all over everything. Judi, in her rudimentary Bahasa Indonesian language told the men that it was "Mrs. Belanger" and they would look at me, laugh, and continue to write Mr. Belanger on the boxes. This infuriated Judi. She told Lestari to tell them, and I could hear Lestari say "yes, madame" and then roll her eyes, trying to figure out how she was going to explain the situation. She did and then the men all started to laugh, which almost drove Judi around the bend. As my mother was so fond of telling us, just roll with the punches, which was why all I could do was laugh.

We left Jakarta in 2007 for Wainwright, Alberta. We went from an archipelago of 34 million to a town of 3,400. Judi was not particularly fond of this posting, and luckily for Judi's sake, we only stayed for ten months. I was not happy to leave there though as I loved Wainwright — the work anyway. Wainwright Detachment belonged to 1 MP Regiment in Edmonton and was a very small detachment, with only approximately seventeen people in total, which included one Major. As soon as I arrived on the ground, the Major deployed to Afghanistan, which left me, a seasoned WO, in charge of the guardhouse. I had a Sergeant (Sgt) as my second in charge. This detachment needed a lot of love, and I was just the person to give it to them. I wanted to try out my new leadership approach, and I could hardly wait. We went from the worst detachment in the regiment to the model detachment for 1 MP Regiment in less than one year. Morale was high, and people volunteered to come in on days off to help other shifts if they were short, or simply to aid in a search of a suspect's premises. As one of the smallest detachments in the regiment, we were producing the most results for the regiment, which led people to wonder how Wainwright could go from a sleepy hollow the year before to the bustling base this year. The answer was simple: servant leadership. I got to practise what I had been shown for the last four years in Asia, and the result was amazing — or at least I thought it was. We were productive, people were happy, and people wanted to come to work.

So why, not even a year after I left, did the guardhouse fall apart again? The answer is simple — it was my fault! I failed to share the knowledge I had, which when I left, triggered a lack of consistency on how decisions were made, how problems were handled, and how subordinates were led. When I heard the news about the Det almost having its doors closed and having to go through an audit, I was angry. I could not figure out how we went from the model detachment to almost being shut down. I didn't have to look far for the answer. I was the problem. I was the boss, answerable to someone two hours away, and this gave me the freedom to use my new leadership approach with impunity. In other words, I did not have to justify it to the officer, because he was gone. The problem was, I didn't quite fully know what I was doing yet with this newfound leadership approach. Production just simply was not enough. I needed to develop my people because growing them into leaders would help contribute to the team.

While I knew I was successful, my success didn't translate into team success. I failed to develop my subordinates to grow in a way that I had. I didn't do this for any nefarious reason. I tried to replicate a style of leadership that I thought was a good fit for me, without fully understanding it first to see if this was actually the leadership style best suited for me.

I was a production leader and I thought if I was producing, then the whole team wins. Nobody won in the Wainwright case. I continued to use this style in Esquimalt, but here, I had officer oversight and did not have the free hand I had in Wainwright. In 2011, I read John C. Maxwell's The 5 Levels of Leadership. I could not put this book down. It was the best leadership book I had ever read! I used the knowledge I gained from Randolf Mank, the Canadian Ambassador to the Embassy in Jakarta, Jonathan Yendall, the senior political officer, and Cindy Munro, who ran the Immigration Section, and finally understood where I went wrong in Wainwright. Instead of developing people, I was stuck on the production leader level, and this helped no one.

This book changed the way I approached leadership, and I became a level 5 leader trying to create a level 5 organization. But when I had the rank and the position to affect change, I was up against an institution that did not want to change. I wanted to create opportunities that others didn't have, but I had to fight through the other leaders who simply wanted the status quo to remain. This created a huge crack in my armour because I knew what it took for me to get to this leadership level, so I could not understand why others, who were at the same rank, were not acting with their subordinates' best interests at heart. My trust and belief in what I thought was a great institution started to diminish at this point. It made me angry, and I needed a release for this pent-up frustration. Unfortunately, I took that anger out on Judi.

Immediately upon our return to Canada I booked a medical appointment and had a full physical. I explained to the doctor the problem I was having with my legs but, unfortunately, she did not figure out the problem. She did however discover that my white blood cell was extremely high. A high blood cell count means you either have a current infection or you have cancer. I didn't have an infection! This concerned me because my mother had been diagnosed with breast cancer while we were posted to Jakarta. There was no time for follow up by the doctor because we were posted less than one year after arriving in Wainwright.

Cyprus and Returning Home (2007–2008)

In 2008, we were off to Esquimalt, BC. It was here where we became empty nesters for the first time. One child went off to university while the other decided to remain in Wainwright. It was also here where I deployed again. This time it was in support of Canadian troops coming off the battlefield in Afghanistan to acclimatize themselves before going home to their loved ones.

Cyprus was an interesting deployment as I was responsible for the MP Detachment for Afghanistan Support at the Third Location Decompression (TLD) in Pathos. The other TLD support staff were all from Kingston, while the MP hailed from all across Canada. The Company Sergeant Major (CSM), the Financial Officer, and the Supply Technician (SUP TECH) were all curious as to what I looked like, so they admitted to me that they stalked me on Facebook to see who I was. I was not and still am not on Facebook, although I do hide behind my wife's social media account and creep her posts.

When I deployed to Cyprus, it was with Rotation (ROTO) 5.5 and 6, and despite 5 MP ROTOs going before us, we were the only MP Detachment to finish all our MP files before the soldiers were sent back in Canada. This meant that soldiers who had broken regulations could be punished in theatre. We also were the only detachment to establish Standing Orders for the MP Section — complete all other tasks assigned to us. Notwithstanding all this, no recognition was to come.

Our deployed role was to police Canadian soldiers, and we did not have jurisdiction outside of that. This was an important distinction because one of my investigators and I almost got arrested by the local police for investigating a crime against one of our people that the civilian police refused to look into. We decided we would help them, which was a bad move — they didn't want our help.

Of course, my arrogance didn't help the situation either. I walked into "their house" and flashed my badge at them, knowing full well that they were not issued one and that it was a sore spot with them. I attempted to emasculate them, and it backfired on me. It almost cost my second in command, who was also the National Investigation Service (NIS) investigator attached to my section, his freedom that night.

We were detained at their police station for a couple of hours before I called in a favour and telephoned my friend from the Cypriot Secret Police. He walked into the police station, and two minutes later we were free to go. Can you just imagine the embarrassment to Canada — members of their own police force arrested by another police force!

I was still having issues with my legs, and by this time I could barely pass a military PT test. Again, they did not find anything. I still wasn't sleeping at night, and now not only were my legs tired, but I had developed this incessant need to move them constantly once I laid down. I was becoming more and more frustrated with the medical system.

It was extremely easy for me to access booze without Judi there to cast judgment. The MP Guardhouse had their own drinking establishment on base, and I used to call "sliders" every Friday at noon. Sliders are what the Navy calls having the afternoon off. I would get in trouble when I got home, but by then I didn't care because I was already drunk. If she dared to say anything while I was drunk it would be like World War III. Despite being the MWO in Charge of the Military Police Guardhouse, I still faced discrimination from the naval Chiefs on the base. No matter where I went, I seemed to face a level of discrimination that my male counterparts did not have to face. It was like I had to prove myself capable. My credibility was always in question, but the men's credibility was not. It drove me nuts. Sometimes, these men would open their mouths and go on about something they did not know about and still maintain their credibility. If I was to do exactly that, I would have lost my credibility (assuming I had accumulated some), and that loss would have followed me to other postings.

In Esquimalt, I continued to hone my leadership skills, but this time I understood that I had to develop the people I worked with. I had to not only work with them but I needed to share my knowledge so they could replicate the work. And they did. Once again, a mediocre detachment fought its way to the top using a leadership style that served others before themselves.

After Esquimalt came Toronto. Luckily for me all the more experienced MWOs did not want to live in Toronto, so they declined the position, and I was asked to take it. It was an awesome opportunity because all the other MP Regiments were run by Chief Warrant Officers except Toronto and Gagetown. Gagetown was fairly small, so it made sense to have a MWO there, but the Toronto Detachment of 2 MP Regiment was big. I was being given an opportunity to show off what I had learned in Jakarta as a new MWO in a senior position.

Unfortunately, from a personal perspective, Toronto was extremely tough on my relationship with Judi because my legs were almost always exhausted, and when I got home from work, I just wanted to lie on the couch. Judi could not understand why I could do PT at work but I couldn't find the energy to even walk the dog at home. I was suffering from an injury that couldn't be seen. I had been going to the doctor at every posting since 2007, complaining of the same issues, but it was not until a female doctor in Toronto sent me to a specialist in 2011 that I was diagnosed with peripheral artery disease (PAD). I had very little oxygen going to my legs because both my iliac arteries were significantly blocked. The specialist also found that I had the beginning of coronary artery disease (CAD). It took four years from the time I returned to Canada and began complaining of these symptoms to diagnose me with PAD and CAD. I was put on entry-level medications for high cholesterol and high blood pressure. Even though they found the beginning of CAD, I did not receive follow-up care for this disease, and sometime between then and 2022 I had a silent heart attack and needed a stent put in my right coronary artery. Furthermore, my entry-level medications were never checked or changed in eleven years, even though every time I would go to the military hospital, my blood pressure would be through the roof.

For the longest time I was angry at Judi for the way she reacted when I had these symptoms with my legs. I had a very hard time forgiving her, and this almost cost us our relationship. But in some sober moments, I would think back on everything I had done to her that she had forgiven me for, and I didn't have the heart to leave. Due to serving Canada before myself, I was posted every one to two years, and as a result never had steady medical care. Naturally, when I would go to the doctor, they would want to start at ground zero. By the time they got up to speed on my medical condition, I would be posted again, and the cycle would repeat itself. In fact, during my first Borden posting (1993–2000) the pressure squeezing my heart was so intense that the only way I could relax was to have my wife rub my back and then sleep on my stomach. These manifested physical symptoms became so bad, I was afraid to leave the airport in Edmonton for Cold Lake, Alberta, because the drive from the airport to 4 Wing was very long and remote and I was convinced that I would have a heart attack and we would be too far from a hospital to save me. I think these were my responses to fight-or-flight syndrome. The problem was that my anxiety put me in a chronic state of hyperarousal, even when there were not any real dangers to fight or flee from. Over time this chronic anxiety either led to or exacerbated my high blood pressure because my heart was always racing. I was in a state of chronic tachycardia. I also believe the elevated levels of stress that were part of my military life caused my chronic high cholesterol.

◆ ◆ ◆

Deploying is never easy on a couple, but it is how you choose to reunite and move forward together with new routines that will make or break your relationship. Moving from location to location is also never easy on a couple, especially when there are children involved and the civilian spouse has a really good job. Being transferred to a new location or even being deployed is easy for the military member because all we do is change offices; everything else stays relatively the same. It is not the same for our spouses and children. They have to give up everything they know to follow you. I asked a great deal from my family, but I forgot to say thank you until it was almost too late. Despite learning this new leadership style, I did not practice it at home.

    I concentrated on figuring out how I was going to employ servant leadership at work, which occupied a great deal of my time. I knew the way I was leading in Canada before spending four years in Jakarta was wrong, but I just didn't know any other way to lead until I watched Ambassador Randolf Mank and Cindy Munro operate. I promised myself that I would be a leader that people could respect, just like them.

Intuitively, when I saw servant leadership being carried out, I knew I needed to first learn, then practice, and finally lead subordinates using this style. When I failed in Wainwright, it almost devastated me. I was a changed person, at least at work, but I still let people down. In my mind, good leaders never let their people down. Not only was I ashamed of myself for the way I treated people before I left Canada, but my failure in Wainwright became one of the biggest regrets in my career. These people counted on me to take care of them, and I let them down.

Despite everything else that was going on in our life, Judi became my biggest advocate at this point because she could see how much I had grown as a leader. She could see that no matter the situation, I would never compromise the institution's trust in me. The system promoted me to the rank I was, and I was determined to show the system that it was not wrong to promote me. I could and would put the institution before my own personal needs. She often told me that the institution needed me to fight for those who could not fight for themselves. While that was true, it became a huge burden because in the end I didn't have the strength to even fight for myself, let alone for others.

10
LOUDERSHIP VS LEADERSHIP

Why are you leading? Is it to be served, or to serve?
— *Ken Blanchard*

TRYING TO SURVIVE in a male-dominated environment that wanted nothing more than to expel me from its midst took a heavy toll. The constant struggle to have a voice, to be heard, and to be seen forced me to act in ways I was not proud of. Faking a leadership style that did not match my core identity did not help either. In the beginning of my leadership journey I was trying to lead like my counterparts, by being inflexible, by using the "my way or the highway" authoritarian style, and forgetting to focus on the growth and well-being of my subordinates.

Like Meatloaf, who would do anything for love, I would do anything to fit in. I was trying to show my counterparts that I was one of them. I wanted to be accepted as a soldier in this great institution, and I was willing to do anything for acceptance. When I look back there is little wonder why that Unit CWO threw my WO rank slip-ons at me and said I did not deserve the promotion. I did not deserve them, plain and simple. I was a terrible leader and I knew I needed to change. There was another reason he threw my ranks at me: he was homophobic and his hatred of me was palpable. That was his problem, not mine. It was never easy to deal with him, but I found if I just focused on my principles I could manage when I had to be around him.

According to CWO Dan Campbell, 1 Canadian Air Division CWO, Royal Canadian Air Force, after pondering the question of

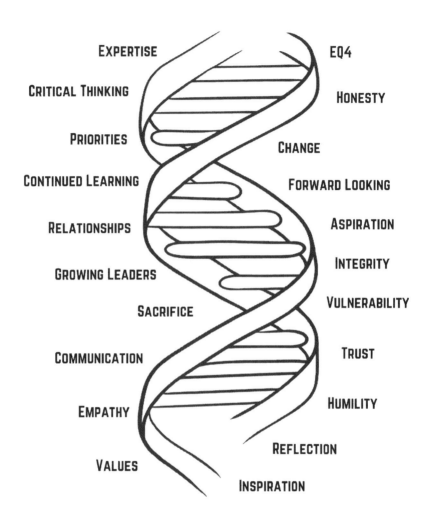

LEADERSHIP DNA

Diagram created by and used courtesy of CWO Daniel Campbell, 1 Canadian Air Division.

why leaders are unique from each other, he came to the conclusion that if there was such a thing as leadership DNA, then individuals could design their own code. CWO Campbell designed a generic code below, based on who you are and how you lead. According to his diagram depicted below, I needed focus on my competence, commitment, and character to create trust with my subordinates.

CWO Campbell posits that in contrast to genetic DNA, Leadership DNA can be developed by the individual, shaped and improved over time with input from many systems. Experience, environment, relationships, successes, and failures all shape an individual's leadership DNA. He concludes that it is in the sequencing that makes each leader different and the fact that as leaders we can write our own code. Your DNA needs to be highly diversified and adaptable to you. Most importantly, your heart has to be in the right place; that you need the disposition to lead for the right reasons and to serve other people and not to be served. The key, however, is that we need feedback from people around us because they know how our behaviour lands with them.

From 2003 to 2007, I changed my leadership DNA. Those four years in Jakarta were incredible for me because I had been provided with an unexpected opportunity to rewrite my own code. I was able to break free from a military dominated environment in order to have the opportunity for new and diverse experiences that jumpstarted the rewrite of my leadership DNA code. And it could not have come at a more opportune time. Despite trying desperately to fit in up to that point in my career, I quickly discovered that not even my military chain of command nor my military superiors would correct or stop public, hostile displays and micro-aggressions against me. Not only was it systemic, but it was also pervasive and culturally embedded within the chain of command. Even if the chain of command wasn't homophobic, they were at least willfully blind to homophobic behaviour. There was no escape for me, no safe place. It was like trying to walk across a minefield without a map.

My entire philosophy on leadership took a 180-degree turn after settling into a new work environment in Jakarta. When someone takes a chance on me and trusts me, I will do everything in my power to never disappoint them. For example, the Canadian Armed Forces took a substantial risk on us, sending us to a country that frowned upon same-sex relationships. I believe we represented our country with poise and grace and that the majority of people outside of our immediate professional and personal space had no idea that homosexuals were living and working amongst them.

When I got my posting, an MP who had already experienced a deployment with Foreign Affairs thought it important to tell me about their experiences with Canadian diplomats. It was evident from their recollections that the MP did not enjoy their time at the embassies they were posted to. Their experience was that the Canadian diplomats were weak in their leadership skills. The MP justified this perspective by stating that the Canadian diplomats never made decisions. According to them, the diplomats would procrastinate until everyone forgot about the decision that had to be made and what they were supposed to be doing. This MP experience was so vastly different from my own. Under the leadership of the Canadian Ambassador to Indonesia, I witnessed some of the greatest leaders I had ever seen. Jonathan Yendall, who was one of the political officers, was very intelligent and had a natural ease about him in leading effectively. He always had a smile on his face and would be the first one to offer his assistance if you were struggling. His charismatic personality caused people to flock to him.

The one person who had the most effect on me, not only as a person but as a leader, was Cindy Munro. Cindy was a very young woman who was already the head of her own department. She ran the Immigration Section. Her quiet confidence and self-assuredness were infectious. She and I were extremely different. We probably would not have been friends had we met in Canada, which would have been a huge loss for me. Being posted abroad, particularly at a hardship post, tends to make people more open to friendships with a more diverse set of people because we all need to recreate social networks to replace (at least temporarily) the ones we left behind. Your potential friendship pool is quite small, which then forces you to be a bit more forgiving in putting up with negative behaviours in order to have friends. At an embassy, we tend to view other Canadians at post almost as an extended family network, with newer arrivals relying on more experienced colleagues for direction and advice in navigating the new environment. Going through crises together further reinforces those bonds. Many of those friendships quickly fade after people leave post, but we have remained friends, despite how unlikely a friendship this was at the outset.

 I watched Cindy closely and knew that this woman had carved out her niche in the workplace. She was comfortable in her own skin, and it showed in everything she did. I wanted to be like her. The other thing that became readily apparent was that she was one of the smartest people I had ever met. Not only was she very smart but she was also very humble. Despite how busy she was, running her own department, she did not hesitate to offer her help when I enrolled in university so I could upgrade my education. Not once did she make me feel stupid, but rather her gentleness in teaching made me want to strive to do better after every submission. I sought her approval and praises because I looked up to her so much. She lifted me up, and although she did not know it, I always felt that I could be my authentic self with her.

 She is an amazing leader, and she makes those around her better. I learned a tremendous amount from her, including how to be a good friend. I credit her with much of my renovation as a person and as a leader because she demonstrated what "right" looked like. Despite being a civilian, I would let her to lead me in to battle any day because she is so trustworthy.

 I was also very fortunate to experience the leadership style of Randolf Mank. He was the Canadian Ambassador to Jakarta from 2003 to 2006. He once told me that one of the toughest responsibilities a good leader needs to learn is to delegate. He expounded on this by explaining that delegation allowed subordinates to grow, to facilitate teamwork, to provide autonomy, and that delegation always led to better decision-making. He said if I learned to do this, I would always have trust with my followers and teammates. This would especially come into play the higher up the leadership ladder I climbed and the more I practised this type of leadership, which I came to learn was called servant leadership.

This simple statement changed my entire philosophy on leadership. But what is extremely ironic is that later in my career, LGen Hood told me the exact same message. No longer did I need to practise a leadership style that did not fit with my personality. From my perspective, Ambassador Mank lead with a deft hand; I immediately knew that I wanted to lead in the same manner.

Naturally, I made some mistakes while learning to exercise this new style of leadership. One of the biggest lessons to learn was knowing exactly what delegation meant and properly exercising it so that I could turn my own productivity into leadership by showing others how to take the reins and run with something. This became blatantly evident in Wainwright, when I failed to delegate. I did the tasks myself and gave credit to the patrolmen, but never really showed them how to do it. I realized too late that they didn't want the credit, they wanted to know how to do it on their own. They realized that one day I would be gone and that they would no longer be able to rely on me to do it for them. Wainwright remains one of my biggest regrets. I squandered an opportunity to make a huge difference in these people's professional journey and I carried that shame for a long time.

The hardest things for me to learn and practise with this style of leadership was to listen well and to understand that leadership DNA guarantees that no two leaders are exactly the same. I was carving my own DNA strand. Understanding people through listening helped me to empathize and connect with them. Instead of waiting for them to finish talking so I could talk, I had to train myself to hear and understand what they had to say. This built trust between us. The major thing I took away from this leadership style was that the subordinates I had the privilege of leading were at the top of the hierarchy and I was at the bottom, responsible for ensuring they were taken care of.

The more I learned about this leadership philosophy the more I was convinced that this would be the best fit for me. Anything had to be better than what I had been doing up to that point. Asking the head of Trade if he was "fucking retarded" because he could not open his DASCO lock and not understanding that this was wrong was not something that you would do under this new leadership style.

I am so fortunate that Judi insisted on me asking the career manager for an Out of Canada (OUTAN) posting, otherwise I would have most likely continued to lead in a transactional manner and not have had the opportunity to watch people like Daniel Campbell, Johnny Ellis, Sandra Bouchard, Geoff Rusconi, Frederick Nolin, Simon deHaerne, Mieszko Jachyra, and Brenda Leroux, to name a few, excel with a little bit of coaching, mentoring, and sponsoring on my part.

Without the likes of Randolf Mank, Jonathan Yendall, and especially Cindy Munro, I probably would not have been the change agent or the mentor I was during my career. Embassy staff, both Canadian diplomats and locally engaged staff, accepted us with open arms. I never forgot the lessons taught to me in Jakarta, and I continued to employ these lessons right up until the day I took off my uniform for the last time.

Up to this point in my career, I was moving along at a normal pace, being promoted a couple of years after entering the promotion zone (EPZ), however, once I adopted the servant leadership philosophy, my career really took off. Suddenly, I was being promoted as soon as I would EPZ, and people were lining up to work with me. I had gained a reputation of unselfishly serving my team and the organization first. I took great pride in the fact that I was known for not using others to prioritize my own objectives.

I became fixated on empowering those who worked with me. I was obsessed at trying to unlock their potential and align their sense of purpose within the CAF ethos. I vowed that no young leader, but especially female leaders, would ever have to go through what I did, and was still fighting right up to my retirement. For anyone who either attended my Change of Appointment ceremony or watched it online, they will know that I was still fighting to have these women recognized for the leaders they were or are or even will be in the future.

Rewriting my DNA leadership code from transactional to servant leadership, I helped them navigate the treacherous waters known as inequity. I had strong views about inequality that included sexual and gender diversity, especially because of my experience. I spent my career pushing for equal representation. Today we are more integrated along gender lines than ever before in our history. Women have been able to serve in every occupation in the CAF since 2000, although the total number of serving women remains around 16 percent of the total force. The percentage of women in senior levels is significantly smaller than at lower ranks, and in my opinion, we will never make it to the government's desire of 25 percent of the CAF being women if we do not start promoting and employing women in senior NCM and officer ranks within the CAF.

To help promote women to higher levels, I always ensured they were the nucleus of the team. I was never the focal point. After committing to this leadership style, I had a vision for each position I went into. It was my belief that this helped subordinates to learn and grow while bringing their own expertise and vision to the table. It was a delicate balance because the whole thing hinged on building influence and bolstering authority rather than using control and toxic leadership tactics. My mentee list almost doubled initially and then tripled once my reputation as a servant leader made its ways around the CAF.

Some peers and superiors, however, made the mistake of thinking that I was weak for using this style of leadership. They tried to walk over me and quickly learned I wasn't the pushover they thought I was. I might choose to not fight back for myself, but if you went after or mistreated one of my subordinates, I never hesitated to stand up and defend them. Simply because I chose to listen to the team and employ suggestions that were made did not mean I could not lead. I chose to lead this way so I could tap into my subordinates' potential. Being a servant leader was a long-term investment. It has been an absolute pleasure in retirement to watch those I empowered advance and prosper in this great organization.

One of those individuals is CWO Sandra Bouchard. While I was the 2 MP Regiment Sergeant-Major in Toronto, I met a young woman who had changed trades from a Combat Engineer to become a Military Policewoman. There was something about this young MCpl that reminded me of me. She was a little rough around the edges, and I wanted to mentor her. I gained her permission to mentor her, and together we set a career path for her, which she followed to the letter.

Upon my behest, she went to the Canadian embassy in Jakarta, Indonesia, for four years. Before she departed, I provided her with a small gift, which was the leadership book by John C. Maxwell. I was recounting this story to a friend when he told me that it is called "paying it forward." He went on to tell me that this is what would happen if 50 percent of the CAF were women. They would mentor people who remind them of themselves just as men have done in the military for decades. The problem is we don't have enough women in the CAF to make this an enduring thing like it is with men. Men do the same thing, but the issue is that they don't privilege women because they are not like themselves. If they did mentor a young woman, they would be chastised for grooming her for ulterior (unethical) motives. This doesn't surprise me, considering the current toxic culture the CAF finds itself in today.

Coming out of the embassy, Sandra was promoted to MWO, then assumed a position as the Unit RSM for the Gagetown MP Detachment within 2 MP Regiment. I even brought her over to CFINTCOM to help the Canadian Forces National Counterintelligence Unit (CFNCIU) move from being under control of the MP Branch to becoming a separate occupation and falling under full control of the Intelligence Branch.

She quickly rose through the ranks and is now a senior appointed CWO, who will be employed summer 2023 as the Strategic Joint Staff (SJS) CWO. If you recall, the SJS CWO is one of the most strategic jobs for CWOs in the CAF. The CWO's main function is to help the Director of Staff in supporting the Chief of Defence Staff and his military advisor role to the Prime Minister of Canada. I tell this story in hopes that men who read it will start mentoring women that they see potential in — just like they do with men.

11

The Lonely Walk to the Fifth Floor

Nothing in this world can torment you as much as your own thoughts.
— *Samantha Gluck*

JAMES COYNE, CO-AUTHOR of Evita Burned Down Our Pavilion, once said that "the shrinks call it post-traumatic stress disorder. I call it hell. The demons are waiting in each corner, ready to drag me back to the battlefield." The worst part of having mental health issues is the stigma attached to them, especially self-stigma, which refers to the negative attitudes, including internalized shame, that people with mental illness have about their own condition. The lonely walk to the fifth floor of the Montfort Hospital, where the psych ward is located, is a prime example. Every time I got in the elevator and pushed the fifth-floor button, I felt like I could hear the others in the elevator saying, "She doesn't look like she's crazy." "I wonder why she is going to the psych ward?" Then the judging: "Just another woman who can't handle her own shit!" Anyone who has had to take this ride can most likely relate to what I am talking about. Getting into the elevator and taking that long ride up to the psych ward tormented my thoughts and made me feel as if I was descending into the bowels of hell, rather than rising to my salvation.

Thinking back, I believe the start of my post-traumatic stress disorder (PTSD) began when I was growing up in the late 1960s and early 1970s and realized I was different from everyone else. The existential threat to my very existence was the attitudes of society toward homosexuals. Hiding in plain sight became essential. For a little girl, these threats really stung because that little five-year-old girl knew that there was something not right with her. When she was treated differently or avoided like the plague, she became convinced that she was exactly what society indicated she was, an aberration.

Looking back on the worst aggressions of my childhood, the one that hurt the most was when my dad took my little television away from me for skipping work to go swimming with my friends and then sold it because, according to him, liars like me didn't deserve nice stuff like that.

This stung more than my dive off the pier. He rarely told us or showed us kids that he was proud of us, so this TV meant the world to me. Perhaps if I had never dove off that pier and smashed my face in, things might have turned out differently, who knows. I just could not contemplate how someone could love you one minute and then abuse you the next. This was too complex of a trauma for a little girl to comprehend. Thus, the consequences of having an abusive father had long-term emotional ramifications on me. Emotionally, I suffered from low self-esteem and a sense of worthlessness. As a defence mechanism, I developed a more aggressive mindset and outlook, though I never hit anyone. My father could never say the same. I often wondered when he looked at us as adults if he regretted beating the shit out of us when we were too conditioned to be obedient to fight back. I wonder, if as an old man, he ever worried that my brother would do to him what he did to us or whether each of us would do the same to our own children.

The other major part of my life that contributed to my PTSD diagnosis came when I joined the Canadian Armed Forces. It was a time when homosexuals were hunted by the system. If they found out a person was gay, they would expel that person from the CAF. Survival became my only hope and success my only revenge for all the wrongs I had suffered — and they were many. For those who told me I should have been exterminated with the Jews, for those who told me they could "fuck the gay out of me," for those who promised a transfer of my choice for a blowjob, and for those who thought it was their right to sexually assault me, my success in achieving Command Chief Warrant Officer status was sufficient revenge for me. Or so I thought. Sadly, all these previous wrongs seemed almost bearable until I joined the Command Chief's highest inner council. Being the only female in that group of eleven Command Chiefs was difficult enough, but it was the two most senior Chiefs within that inner circle whose marginalizing behaviour made it the worst for me.

No one would have guessed that I was suffering in silence and that I had been pretending to be fine for thirty-five years. I wanted to leave the CAF without anyone knowing the cost of my journey through adversity. I tried to carry on with the charade, but the last three years of my career caused me to question everything I believed in about the Canadian Armed Forces and our military ethos. It was just too much to take. It felt like the greatest love of your life had been lying to you for most of your marriage. It was a betrayal of trust.

As one of the highest-ranking enlisted leaders in the Canadian Armed Forces, I should have been in a position where my voice had the most influence, and yet, it had none. I believe that is part of why I am suffering. I am mourning my career. I was not able to achieve my goals as a change agent inside the CAF because I was silenced by a senior Chief who preyed upon my weaknesses. I wonder if you recall alluding to the fact that I was not as good a leader as the others? I obviously do! How about the time you told the entire CWO Corps that the only reason I was there was to keep the rest of you in line when we spoke about culture? Even when you were called out on this misstep you did not apologize or even acknowledge that you said it. Worst of all was during my last month of service, when you invited me to mentor on a Senior Appointment Course. Knowing I was leaving the Forces in less than a month, you took that opportunity, in front of the next generation of CAF NCM leaders, to thank and praise the VCDS Gp CWO for his excellent stewardship of the CAF since he became a CWO. He was taking his commission that summer and leaving the CWO Corps. I apparently did not merit that same praise from you, even though I was also leaving the CWO Corps, which I am sure you had a hand in. By doing this you clearly indicated that I was less important than the VCDS Gp CWO or yourself, and that I did not deserve your respect. You figuratively slapped me directly in the face. The cost of what you and others like you did to me was expensive. You just happened to be my last straw.

I was, however, spared humiliation by the Canadian Special Operations Force Command CWO, CWO Gary Grant, and the Canadian Army Sergeant Major, CWO Jim Smith, who immediately jumped up after you had finished praising your buddy, and stood in front of the entire SAP class, paying me some very nice compliments as a leader. These two men made my last year bearable. They supported me, protected me, and most importantly, they functioned as my sounding board when I needed to vent. CWOs Grant and Smith are two of the most inclusive leaders I have ever met, and they go out of their way to ensure everyone on their team has a voice. Both of these gentlemen understand they possess male privilege, but they make sure to examine this privilege in every decision they make or every piece of advice they give. I am so proud to know them and so very fortunate to have had the opportunity to serve with these two phenomenal leaders.

Every time I was subjected to other misogynistic behaviours and attitudes, I would flashback to the night my attacker ground his penis into my groin. Then, the stress response would kick in and my body would naturally follow the path that best suited itself at the time, either fight, flight, or freeze. By the time I made it to the CWO rank, my "suit of armour" was so heavy I could barely walk when it was on, which was all the time. Besides the obvious, there is an increasing body of evidence that demonstrates how the increased allostatic load, which is defined as "the wear and tear on the body" accumulates when someone is exposed to repeated or chronic stress.

For the most part, I remained silent and towed the party line because I thought leading by example would bring about change, or at least that was what I told myself to help deal with my cowardliness. I again used my old friend, alcohol, to help me accept the lack of respect I had for myself. The first couple of drinks would initially cause me to relax, and those unwanted emotions like depression and anxiety would slowly start to slip away. Unfortunately, after a couple more drinks, that feeling of temporary peace normally gave way to anger and feelings of suicide. I felt like a fraud. I doubted my abilities, despite all the accolades that came my way from respectful superiors and subordinates. I felt like I was fooling everyone who thought I was an excellent leader and mentor, and that only compounded my feelings of not being worthy enough, thus feeding my imposter syndrome and heightening my PTSD.

Feelings of self-doubt ate away at my consciousness and left me feeling insecure and incompetent, despite evidence to the contrary. Regardless of what others said about me, I felt like a phony. When self-doubt crept in, I believed I did not deserve any of the successes I had achieved. I was stuck in a vicious circle and could not find a way to stop the spinning, so I just drank, hoping to numb the pain and forget for awhile.

I also felt like a fraud at home too. I was a terrible parent, who was never around for the children's extracurricular activities because I was usually too busy working, trying to make sure that the institution could not ignore me. What very few people knew and what I counted on, which was "nobody knows what goes on behind closed doors," was that I often drank every weekend and then would lose my temper with my wife and children. To this day my children are afraid when I raise my voice. Every time I would perceive a threat or a slight from my wife, I would engage in aggressive behaviour that would push her away. I often threatened to leave her. Outwardly, I came across as conceited and self-assured, but on the inside, I suffered from low self-esteem because of the shame I carried around constantly. I pushed myself to work as hard as possible because of my feelings of inadequacy. I was never satisfied and always felt that my work could be better. Rather than focus on my strengths, I tended to fixate on my flaws or any mistake I would make. Unless I was drinking, then it was a different story. I became boastful and very overconfident, bragging about my accomplishments and speaking poorly of those who I felt were holding me back.

When sober, I was a humble leader who was extremely ashamed of herself. For years I could not look at myself in the mirror. I hated the person who looked back at me. When drunk, I would constantly look at myself in any surface that allowed me to see my reflection, although I did not know I did this. During a very candid discussion with my wife, she mentioned it and said I would even make faces at myself. After thinking about it for a while, I believe I did it because what reflected back was a surprisingly attractive and funny individual, someone completely different from who I saw when sober, or at least that is what I thought. That is not what my wife saw.

As good as I was perceived to be by others at being a leader and producing material to improve the NCM Corps, I was invisible to my peers. As a woman, I was not good at self-branding. Throughout my career I watched as others would talk about their successes and strengths, letting their bosses know what they had achieved. I did not do this and believe if I did, it would have been perceived completely different. Moreover, as a "pleaser" I let my self-worth be defined by what others thought of me and the things I had accomplished, rather than what was inside of me. I constantly wondered what people were thinking about me, and because of that I did things that made others happy, regardless of my own feelings, but then I would become passive-aggressive about what I already agreed upon.

I recently learned of a study called The Tallest Poppy,[1] whose conclusions fit me to a tee. According to the study, 77 percent of women downplay their own achievements, 72.4 percent are being left out or ignored, 70.7 percent are being undermined, 68.3 percent have their achievements dismissed, and 66.1 percent of women have others taking credit for their work.

My psychologist taught me that making myself happy was more important than pleasing others and to understand my self-worth. I

---

[1] "The Tallest Poppy," Woman of Influence, accessed 1 October, 2023, www.womenofinfluence.ca/tps.

could no longer let it be determined by how people saw me. With her help, we delved into who I was at my core and determined my self-worth from there.

Again, as good as others saw me, what I saw reflecting back at me in the mirror was an imposter. Even when I occasionally demonstrated strength and ambition, micro-aggressions and stereotyping would often ensure I was put right back in my box, where I was presumed to belong. It is no wonder I constantly doubted my abilities, which made me feel like a fraud. The truth was I did not belong because I was never supposed to belong.

I am almost certain there are people who think they know me and would have never guessed that this happened to me. I had buried that genie so deep inside my soul she could not see the light of day for the longest time. I didn't want others to know what happened to me, so I pretended it didn't. I created a lie inside my head and made my heart believe it. You may be asking yourself why it is coming out now, and I do not blame you as I have asked myself the exact same question — why now? The last three years of my career simply became too much. All the pent-up anger, stress, and injustice over my entire career was percolating to the surface, and I was having a harder and harder time shoving the feelings back down inside. My heart was breaking and my head was screaming at me to let the genie come out, and throughout this period my health was failing as a result of all the stress.

I was in my doctor's office in the spring of 2022, getting a medical examination done, when she asked me a remarkably simple question that caused me to lose control of my emotions. Normally, I was very good at covering up my feelings or using distracting techniques to draw the attention away from me, however Dr. Brownlee was having no part of this. She immediately noticed signs of me becoming emotionally overwhelmed. Slowly, she began to probe my emotional state and quickly realized that the intensity of my feelings outmatched my ability to manage them. The genie was out of the bottle, and despite my best efforts to push her back inside where I felt she belonged, there was no convincing her to get back inside the bottle. I curled into the fetal position in my chair, trying to make myself as small as possible, and completely lost control. Dr. Brownlee waited, and with no judgment in her voice, offered quiet words of encouragement for over an hour while I tried to get myself together.

Thank God she was so intent on taking care of me. She noticed my negative emotions and immediately recognized that mental health therapy would be the only way to sort through the trauma I had experienced throughout my career. Despite there being a national wait time of approximately six to nine months for a psychological assessment, Dr. Brownlee managed to arrange for me to start seeing Dr. Monteiro, a clinical psychologist, less than fourteen days after my breakdown in her office.

Due to the severity of my physical and mental limitations, the CDS directed that I be released for medical reasons and that my release date be scheduled for August 31, 2022. When I opened the CDS's email, I was overcome with emotion. I sat there and cried for an hour. My wife asked what was wrong, but I could not explain the feelings I was having. It was weird because we expected that I would get a medical release for my back due to all the FORCE evaluations I had to undergo as a soldier, but I do not think you can truly prepare for a mental health medical release. I did not work my entire career with the goal of leaving on a medical pension. While my rationale side knows that this is a good thing and there are excellent programs in place to take care of my physical and mental health, leaving the CAF with this release item on my record felt to me as if they had won.

It took a while but I finally figured it out: I was suffering from a series of moral injuries. What was happening within the "famous" inner circle contradicted my own core moral values and behavioural expectations of the others who were occupying seats at this table. I felt it was our collective duty and responsibility to safeguard the pan succession management system. Our job was to ensure it always remained transparent, whereby we could all put hand on heart and state that the appointment went to the right person, with the right qualifications, at the right time, and especially for the right reason.

In several cases, I knew that the right person did not necessarily get the job. Being on the wrong side of the vote in these cases, and yet ultimately going along with the decision, went against my moral beliefs. For the past three years I had been paying the price for having betrayed these people. I stood in front of my subordinates and told them to their faces that the system was fair and equitable. I lied! For those subordinates who have felt betrayed over the last three years, I am sorry. I was not the only one in the circle who felt this way, but unfortunately it only took the agenda of one or two to screw up the guidelines we had in place to keep us honest.

I did not escape my position without feeling the effects of having played a part in individuals' non-selection for specific pan CAF positions. I am still feeling the effects of the role I played in some peoples' demise, especially if their career ended earlier than it should have. The effects of moral injury are worse than being punched in the face over and over and over again. This type of injury hurts your soul. Metaphorically and literally, moral injury almost took my life.

As June 2022 fast approached, I knew my days were numbered. I was about to retire, and I was spiralling out of control. After a long career of pushing the ball up the hill, I failed at the one thing I wanted to accomplish more than anything else — to be an agent of positive change.

The other thing that had me discombobulated was the fact that I needed to share with my family what had been happening to me for the past thirty-five years. It was not fair to continue to keep them in the dark, and furthermore, I could not have them learn of this for the first time when they read my book. I had kept this part of my life separate, secret, and silent. I realized that to move forward in my healing process, my family needed to know why I acted the way I did. My wife had a right to know why I drank to oblivion and then deliberately picked fights with her. She needed to know why, on multiple occasions, I tried to leave her for no reason whatsoever. My children had a right to know why I was never around for them while they were growing up, why everything else in my life seemed to be more important than them, and why I was always criticizing them.

Going through this vulnerable and humbling process I have admitted to myself that when I am at my worst, I am my father's daughter. I have been given a second chance to become the person I see in my mind's eye. When I will be at my best I can proudly proclaim that I am my mother's daughter.

Shortly after commencing mental health therapy, I began to reveal parts of my story to my wife. She was shocked, to say the least, but it helped her understand some of my previous behaviours. She had always been my biggest cheerleader, despite me not being able to see that. She helped raise me up to stand tall when I could not find the strength, and she guided me through the chaos by reminding me of my larger purpose when I would lose sight of why I joined this great institution in the first place. I joined to make change and to be a leader of diversity, equity, and inclusion. I wanted to advance diverse teams because I knew that they make for a stronger fighting force, a more capable force, and a force multiplier across the board. I was taught exceedingly early in my career that my most important role as a NCM leader was to be an expert in the human domain, influencing the day-to-day life of CAF personnel. I had gotten particularly good at having others believe I was doing this, or at least that was what I wanted people to see. Even my wife believed it. However, that one came back to bite me in the ass.

Over the last three years of my career, each time I mentioned retirement she would continue to push me to help those who could not help themselves, to be their voice for change, but what she failed to see or had no way of knowing was that I could not even help myself. I was exhausted. I was worn out. I had been beaten down to the point of surrender. My body and soul were giving out on me. In my last year of service, my assistant Sgt Simon de Haearne carried me and covered for me.

The sexual harassment, the sexual assault, the micro-aggressions, all the backhanded compliments, all the exclusionary tactics used to keep me out, all the interruptions when I was speaking, all the snide comments, all the stealing of my ideas and work, and the blatant exile by ostracism took its toll. I have since learned that they did this for reasons of power, social status, and prejudices. It was not because I could not measure up or because I was "junk," as I was once called, but ultimately, I knew how much more weight I was carrying than them and yet I was still an effective leader.

I might not have been able to control what happened to me, but I could control how I responded. Please know this — everything done to me did not destroy me. I struggled hard to hide the things that were seen by others as imperfections, but thanks to my therapist and a very devoted and loving wife, I have embraced these flaws, because they are what made me the leader I was. Embracing this newfound philosophy made me realize that I needed to convey my CAF journey to my children. I owed it to them, and my opportunity came during the week of my Change of Appointment ceremony. Despite all that I put them through as children, they still dropped everything to be by my side for my retirement. My youngest daughter forewent her own graduation to attend, and my eldest daughter was getting married less than two weeks after my retirement.

I sat them down a couple of days before my retirement ceremony, and with my wife's support, I explained how for my entire life I had believed that I was flawed in some way because I was born a lesbian. And because of this, I was unworthy of love or respect, and I would drive people away from me so they could not hurt me, or I would never allow them to see the real me. I apologized to them for being a terrible parent. I explained what I had gone through in my career and both girls were outraged. The first thing they wanted to know was if their mother knew the entire time, which of course she did not, and that satisfied them. They also wanted to know why I never shared that burden with them before, and then they felt sad for me. I asked them not to pity me. Their pity would only aggravate the pathetic feeling of helplessness and hopelessness that I was already struggling with. As it turned out, this was the best thing I could have done for our family. It brought my eldest daughter, who was always afraid of me when I drank, and who always walked on eggshells around me, closer than we have ever been. My youngest daughter wanted to "beat up" all the people who intentionally hurt me in some way. My wife now has more empathy and compassion for me, and our marriage is better than it has ever been. I also cut way back on my drinking and switched from hard liquor to beer. For the first time in a very long time, I am seeing life through sober eyes.

12
TACTICIAN VS STRATEGIST

Without an effect at the tactical level, the strategic leader is merely creating fiction.
— *CWO Daniel Campbell*

THERE IS SOMETHING VERY SEDUCTIVE about being a tactician. It has noticeably clear responsibilities. Your focus is on the here and now, the today, and the tomorrow, rather than the nebulous possibilities of the long-range future. When I first joined the CAF, I thought I would be lucky to get to the rank of MCpl because I was up against an institution that wanted nothing more than for me to quit, and I was not very obedient either. It seemed that the system did everything in its power to ignore me.

While the CAF had changed in some areas, for example, accepting gay people within their mix and allowing them to serve openly, it still had not changed when it comes to the power imbalance between men and women. The problem with the military profession in general is that it is (and has been for a long time) predicated on power, ego, and tokenism. Power relies on like promoting like — men promoting men. Ego speaks to everyone trying to build a reputation of professional competence to get the promotion and trying not to show weakness or less than perfection. Less than perfection is seen as a criterion to deselect someone for promotion. In essence, we can't fail so we move rapidly to a zero-risk tolerance culture, which leads to hiding mistakes and not learning from them. Tokenism is the practice of making only a perfunctory or symbolic effort to do a particular thing, especially by recruiting a small number of people from underrepresented groups in order to give the appearance of sexual or racial equality within a workforce. Simply put, male dominance is fueling more male leadership. We need to assess on more than just performance — this is where character can come in — and maybe we will get leaders up there with different perspectives, like women, visible minorities, and heaven forbid, support occupations.

Moving from leading people as a tactician, inside of my occupation, to getting the nod to lead the institution as a strategist, did not come without a very expensive price tag attached. In 2012, when I was first selected for senior appointment, the RCAF wanted to send me to Saint-Jean to be the recruit school CWO. I declined because we had been transferred four times in the last five years at that point. It was not fair to ask Judi to live in a province where she could not speak the language and would to be forced to sit at home for three years while I worked.

I was under the impression that they accepted my reasoning for not going to Quebec as they sent me back to school at the Royal Military College (RMC) in Kingston, Ontario, to take part in the non-commissioned member executive professional development programme (NEPDP). I earned a certificate in general military studies from RMC and a bachelor's degree in military arts and science with first class distinction.

Unfortunately, this was a bad assumption on my part because, when I finished school, they wanted to post me right back to Saint-Jean but give me a different job. I refused, and as a result I was then considered "junk," according to some of the inner council members at the time. Some wanted to return me to my Branch as a MP, especially if I was going to be ungrateful about the alleged opportunity!

This was the first time I became consciously aware that I was not part of the "old boys club." Often, it was so subtle that I wondered if I was overthinking things or simply imagining it. I chose to believe that these men did not mean to exclude me, or even realize they were doing it. The fact of the matter is that the dominant male population has served to empower male cultural norms. This is called affinity bias (our tendency to be drawn to people like us). For me, I had a communication style that clashed with theirs because I tended to think more critically. In other words, the status quo was never my friend. I realized that I could touch more people through writing than I ever could in person. My pen could not be silenced like my mouth was every time I did not agree with the majority. I had different expectations for my working relationship with men of the CAF. For the longest time I was not aware that my expectations were not being met — that was until I reached the pinnacle of my success as a Command Chief Warrant Officer in 2019.

Not everyone can make or wants to make the transition from the tactical to the strategic level. Tactical leaders focus on the day-to-day execution of activities. We are trained to do this from day one and are really good at it. Strategic level thinkers are longer-term thinkers and are okay with broad overall direction. I like to think about it as the steward being the strategic thinker, the campaigner the operational thinker, and the operator the tactical thinker.

In 2014, I was appointed to the Strategic Joint Staff (SJS). The SJS is an unusual unit in the CAF. Designed primarily to manage the nexus between the other levers of national security, the day's focus is on supporting the Chief of Defence Staff (CDS) and his military advisor role to the Prime Minister of Canada. It is also a bit unique since the majority of SJS staff are senior officers (majors and above), with only a small number of junior officers and senior NCMs. I was exposed to a great deal of strategic issues, and I got to see a side of the military that not many senior officers got to see, let alone a CWO.

Early on in my tenure as the SJS CWO, the CAFCWO and the Vice Chief of the Defence Staff (VCDS) CWO of the day asked me to brief the CAFCWO inner council on how the SJS worked because very few people understood its role and function. While waiting to brief, I was standing outside Conference Room B on the thirteenth floor of National Defence Headquarters (NDHQ) with a couple of the other Command CWOs, including the RCAF Command CWO. I was extremely nervous as I had never briefed at this level before. I was positive that the RCAF Command CWO could smell my vulnerability and thought he could attack to embarrass me in front of the others. He looked at me with a smirk on his face and said, "We haven't met, who are you?" I made it a point of blatantly looking at the rank on his shoulder and very professionally, and as sweet as I could, replied, "I'm CWO Belanger, and you are?" The other Command CWOs present started snickering, and he spun on his heel and walked away. While his attempt to embarrass appeared to miss the mark at that moment, internally it struck a bullseye. In that instant he made me feel worthless. I did, however, get the last laugh because it seemed I had an affinity for the strategic level.

My boss at the time, the Director of Staff (DOS) of the SJS, Major-General Michael Hood, was instrumental in my success at this level. He was my Command Team partner at the SJS, located in the National Defence Headquarters in Ottawa. The first thing he did to make me feel like part of the team was to open his entire battle rhythm to me. He went on to explain how Canadian National Governance and Strategic Planning worked. He taught me that it is not a linear process and that the Canadian Military never works alone, and most importantly that the higher up you go the less direction you get. He took the time to teach me some extremely valuable lessons about how to operate in Ottawa, which served me well for the remainder of my career. He introduced me to key players within Defence, both inside the Privy Council Office and the Prime Minister's Office, which was a good thing because when I first arrived at that level I would hear people refer to the "Clerk" all the time. I thought the Clerk was a human resource administrator! Who would have guessed they were talking about the Clerk of the Privy Council, the head of the Public Service and the most senior civil servant in the Government of Canada. In addition, every time someone would mention the Chief, I thought they were talking to me or about me and I would answer. Again, who knew they meant the Chief of Defence Staff and not the Chief of the SJS, CWO Belanger!

On a more serious note, MGen Hood was the reason I not

only survived the strategic level but actually thrived in this type of environment. He displayed patience and taught me that while it was crucial to understand the complexities and the interworking of government, my most vital role, regardless of the level I would achieve, was that I needed to be an expert in the human domain, influencing the day-to-day life of CAF personnel. This lesson was the most important of my career. Unfortunately, I only got to stay one year in this position, with this incredible leader, before I was asked to assume the position of the Operation HONOUR CWO and MGen Hood was promoted to Lieutenant-General (LGen) and took over as the RCAF Commander.

When Madame Deschamps's External Review into Sexual Misconduct and Sexual Harassment in the Canadian Armed Forces report for Operation HONOUR came out I was still posted to the SJS. I started to read it and got to about page ten before throwing it in the garbage. I was offended that she would report that the whole institution was rotten. I told myself this was not my experience. I had repressed my assault and all the micro-aggressions against me and somehow managed to convince myself these things never happened to me. After thinking about it for a bit, I pulled the report out of my garbage can, and this time I got maybe halfway through it before throwing it back in the garbage. This time I was really angry because she stated that MP did not know how to investigate properly and that senior NCO women were to blame because they would tell other women to just suck it up. She then accused all senior NCOs of trying to block someone from reporting. I felt like she was attacking me on all three fronts. After a lot of discussions with LGen Hood on this matter, I realized it wasn't about me. I picked up the report again, and this time was able to read the document from start to finish, and although I did not want to admit it, she was right. Then, the offer came. I was being given the opportunity to be Rear Admiral (RAdm) Jennifer Bennett's command team partner at Operation HONOUR. It seemed like a sign from above.

I figured that this job would be an opportunity for me to give back. I was brainwashed into believing that my CAF would never do this to their own women. I had subconsciously blocked out what they did it to me and so many others. I wanted to be there, in any way I could, for those women who had a lot more courage than I ever did, to come forward with their complaints.

I jumped in with both feet and went to work with RAdm Bennett. She was phenomenal. She and I were responsible for trying to change a culture by preventing and addressing sexual misconduct within our ranks. More specifically, my role was to explain the strategic-level thinking and products being produced at this level and then distill that information so that the person on the ground could understand what that meant for them.

While a stressful mandate, RAdm Bennett made it fun to come to work each day. As you can imagine, hearing some of the stories that were being told about sexual misconduct and sexual harassment could get very tough. In fact, as a MP, I had not seen this level of depravity. The best thing that came from me being appointed to this position was that RAdm Bennett taught me to always see the unseen benefit in any situation. She never stopped pushing the ball up the hill, despite our organizational culture trying to stop her. Most importantly, she never stopped smiling and having fun. What an inspiration she was to me and to a lot of other victims of this very toxic CAF culture.

While everyone says Operation HONOUR was a failure, I disagree. I believe we did a good job "flying that plane as we were building it." I do not believe you will ever be able to eradicate sexual misconduct in its entirety. I recall RAdm Bennett and I discussing the CDS's intent to use the word "absolute" in reference to eliminating all sexual misconduct in the CAF. But really, he could not say anything else in that situation. Would you say, "I am going to change the culture by ten percent"? Regardless of the eradication percentage, Operation HONOUR did not fail. It can be credited for the creation of the Sexual Misconduct Response Centre (SMRC) and the beginnings of Respect in the CAF program, both of which have had a tremendously positive impact across the CAF. Trying to change an organization as mammoth as the CAF is not an easy feat. Once the heat and lights are off the suggested change, the institution snaps right back to centre, returning to the culture they are familiar and comfortable with.

In light of sexual misconduct allegations against two of Canada's highest-ranking Commanders, the Acting Chief of Defence Staff (CDS) had no choice but to cancel Operation HONOUR, as it was synonymous with General Jonathan Vance, the former CDS who was charged and eventually pled guilty to one count of obstruction of justice in relation to his sexual misconduct. The Acting CDS created a new CAF Command, entitled the Chief of Professional Conduct and Culture (CPCC), whose mandate was to combine and incorporate any and all activities that deal with culture change across the Department of National Defence (DND) and the CAF. It is the centre of expertise and the single functional authority for renovating defence culture toward military professionalism as expressed in our new CAF ethos.

I believe there is much work that still needs to be done so that the CAF moves the yardsticks from being a toxic and discriminatory workplace to being an employer of choice for Canadians. You simply cannot change hundreds of years of misogynistic practices that get embedded in operant culture as well as codified in traditions. Having said that, it is evident the system is trying to change itself. The creation of Pride Networks on bases and Wings, the implementation of safe spaces and the Sentinel program, gender advisors, and revamped CAF-wide directives are but a few examples of how the CAF is trying to tear down years of male-to-male learned culture passed on generation to generation across many societies. While there has been progress on paper and in policy, there has not been enough progress in practice.

13
THE BIG LEAGUES

It's tough when the institution you love ignores you, but it's even tougher when you feel that you have no choice but to pretend that you don't mind.

— *CWO (Ret'd) Necole Belanger*

HAVING MADE THE POSITIVE CHANGES to my leadership style in 2007 and having had the opportunity to hone the skills of a servant leader over a period of five years paid off in 2014 with an appointment to the Strategic Joint Staff (SJS). This would be my first of five senior appointments that I would hold before my retirement. I had just graduated from the Royal Military College in Kingston. For these positions you compete for a job that is outside of your occupation and outside of your environment, so your file, among others, is presented to the Canadian Armed Forces Chief Warrant Officer (CAFCWO) Inner Council.

Only the environmental Command CWOs of the Navy, Army, Air Force, and Special Forces can bring files forward to the inner council at this time. To be awarded a pan CAF position, you must have the majority of the ten votes. For environmental jobs, it is the Environmental Command CWO and a small panel of personnel chosen by that environment who will determine your fate at this level.

Most people will spend three years in a senior appointment position, whether that is at the tactical, operational, or strategic level. I am not most people apparently! In 2015, my file was again in front of the inner council. This time I was competing for the Operation HONOUR CWO position. Both this job and the SJS job were strategic-level positions.

One year into the job as the Operation HONOUR CWO, I was selected by the RCAF to be the 16 Wing CWO. Located in Borden, Ontario, 16 Wing is known as the birthplace of the RCAF. This position is at the tactical-operational level. After two positions at the strategic level, where I was working with mostly senior officers at the rank of Brigadier General and above, dropping back to the tactical level was a blast. It was so much fun because I had more direct influence over people and I was working on day-to-day issues with immediate outcomes, versus strategic issues where the timelines are much longer. I stayed in this position for two years before moving again. In 2018, I was appointed as the Formation CWO for the Canadian Defence Academy. I loved this job. It felt like it was tailor made for me and I loved coming to work. I was revamping NCM CAF common training and had the utmost trust of my command team partner, RAdm Luc Cassivi. I must have been doing a really good job because others, outside of CDA, were taking credit for my work. I rationalized the hurt by telling myself that I didn't care as long as it got into the hands of those who needed it.

I also worked with LCol Bill Cummings, who was the Officer in Charge of all Professional Development (PD). The LCol gave me his ultimate trust as the expert in NCM PD. We developed a very close working relationship, and when it came time to write this book, there was no one I trusted more. He had a knack of being able to draw passion and real emotion out of me. I was sad to leave this job, but my ego got the better of me. My ultimate job was the VCDS CCWO, and taking the Canadian Forces Intelligence Command (CFINTCOM) CCWO position would get me one step closer to achieving my goal of becoming the VCDS CCWO. So after just one year, I moved again.

In 2019, I was selected as the CCWO for CFINTCOM. I had made it to the CAFCWO's inner council. I had earned my seat at the big-boy table in the CAF for NCMs and I had been drafted into the big leagues. The cost of getting there was expensive, both for my physical and mental health. I should have listened to my inner voice that kept saying, Be careful what you ask for, you just might get it. Giving up a great job at CDA to have zero influence at the strategic level gave me a severe ulcer.

In my first two years on the council, I was simply tolerated, and if I opened my mouth to voice my opinion, I was subjected to indifference. I would rather have been faced with hostility than be totally ignored. I would wager that the majority of the other members of this council did not even realize they were doing this to me. I had one friendly face on the council in those first two years, and that was my good friend CWO Denis Gaudreault. He always had my back, regardless of what his peers thought. Sadly, in order for me to get an idea across, he had to verbally agree with what I was saying and put his support behind my point and then repeat the idea in his own words, otherwise the idea and I would simply get brushed aside.

The members of the CAFCWO inner council are considered the NCM power elite within the CAF, and within the group there is a hierarchy. These elites were a tight-knit group, and I was seen as an outsider because I did not share common backgrounds and positions with these members. Also, CFINTCOM is not necessarily considered to be a "proper" command equal to the others because of its relatively smaller size and function. I watched as the group went mostly unchecked regarding some of the decisions they made; groupthink and status quo was alive and well within this tight cohort.

If you have someone at the top who is more interested in serving their own ego or agenda rather than serving the institution, things can and will go very wrong. In the end, if you are not given the rules of the game, it will be extremely hard, if not impossible, for you to be successful. In the first two years of my membership to this group, I was not given the rules, so the game was not very transparent, and I found that the rules were not the same for all groups. If the game was transparent, and the rules the same for all groups, we should see more diverse individuals occupying the most senior leadership positions within the CWO Corps, but the reality is that we don't.

I ask that you keep in mind that what I am about to say is my perception of reality. As Virginia Woolf so poignantly stated in Three Guineas, "Though we see the same world, we see it through different eyes," So before I get into anything, I will say I believe this is not a pipeline issue but rather a bias issue, specifically a second-generation bias, which for the most part is hidden from view. But I felt it. The result is that women simply don't have the numbers men have in terms of representation.

I mentioned earlier that the ten Command CCWO, along with the CAFCWO, who makes up the eleventh position, are the most powerful and influential NCM in the CAF. When determining who will go forward to represent the institution, it is this group who decides. Command Chief Warrant Officer positions were created in 1978, and since then there have only ever been three women who have held these positions. In 2002, CWO Camille Tkacz became the first woman appointed to a Command CWO position as the CWO for the Assistant Deputy Minister (Human Resources — Military). Fourteen years later, in 2016, CWO Colleen Halpin was appointed as the VCDS Gp CWO. And in 2019, I became only the third woman in CAF history to be appointed as a Command CWO. Today, there is zero representation of women at this level. I believe there is zero representation at this level because they simply change the rules to get the result they want. For example, I believe the rules of the game were changed on three separate occasions, and potentially a fourth, whereby someone's personal agenda got in the way of me having a fair shot at being considered for a position during succession management. The first time it happened to me was when I was nominated for a certain position. I felt like the interviewer was simply going through the motions to speak with me to try to make it appear as if the process was fair. It seemed like the Commander had already made their decision. This feeling also came from people telling me that the Commander's NCM partner had been saying for almost a year that his buddy was going to replace him. That turned out to be the case.

The next time this occurred to me was during the same posting season. I was still at the CDA, however the RCAF felt I was ready to assume a Command CWO position. They nominated me for the VCDS Gp CWO position. In the past, this specific position was the same as all the other Command CWO positions, in that the Army, Navy, Air Force, and Special Forces nominated people who were already holding a position at the Divisional Level but were being considered as a potential Command CWO could compete for this job. Unfortunately, that year a decision was made that this specific position would only be filled by a currently serving Command CWO who would be leaving their position or who wanted the job, because the position was now being coined the "first amongst equals" and a new level was arbitrarily assigned to it. The position was designated, although not officially, as a .5 level position. According to our Strategic Employment Model directive, a .5 level does not exist.

Once this was in place and communicated to the Chief of Defence Staff, a decision was made that a currently serving Command CWO would be chosen to fill the position. No one else was permitted to interview, and the rest of us learned of this new rule once the individual was named and their name was published in a Canadian Forces General message (CANFORGEN) message.

The third time I believe there was a hidden agenda in my case was with the Level 0 position — the CAFCWO position — which had come open unexpectedly in 2020. The customary rule, although not written, was that anyone serving as a Level 1 Command CWO was allowed, if they were interested, to interview for the position. According to a confidential source, General Vance told the RCAF Commander that the RCAF could submit one file. The RCAF's nomination was the currently serving RCAF COMMAND CWO, Denis Gaudreault, as he would soon be finished his three-year term in that position, and I had just started my position as the Command CWO for the Canadian Forces Intelligence Command (CFINTCOM). I was okay with this because, in my opinion, Denis would have made a way better CAFCWO than me.

Once the process was complete and the new CAFCWO chosen,

it was discovered, from an exceptionally reliable source, that General Vance wanted a more diverse panel to choose from, so he asked for a female candidate. I was the only female Command CWO, but it was not me he asked for, it was a Divisional CWO — a Level 2 female CWO. When the RCAF questioned the office of the outgoing Canadian Forces Chief Warrant Office, his apparent response was that I had said when I first became a Command CWO that I did not want his job. Whether I said that to him or not, I still should have been given an opportunity to decline to have my name go forward.

The last post I interviewed for was just before my release in 2022. Again, the position was the VCDS Gp CWO. I agreed to let the RCAF put my name forward for this job despite the rulesets established from 2019. No other serving Command CWO volunteered to have their name go forward for the position. Therefore, based on that 2019 precedence, I should have automatically gotten the position, just like the person vacating the job did. A decision was made to seek out two more nominations from Divisional CWO candidates. Since I am retired, I obviously did not get this job, again! However, I respect the fact that the VCDS sought out other candidates and changed the rules back to what they used to be, which ensures that the right candidate is chosen at the right time, for the right reasons. I cannot have it both ways. I cannot complain when the rules are changed, as they were in 2019, and then complain again in 2022, when the rules are changed back and it does not work in my favour. This was a prime example of the personal cost of ethics. In the end, it is the Commander who decides how many candidates they want to interview. I respect that. What I do not respect, is the assumed role the outgoing VCDS Gp CWO played in the Commander's decision-making cycle to change the ruleset back to 2016.

The biases and personal agendas that keep women from being promoted are mostly only understood and felt by the women themselves. For example, all the micro-aggression I faced in my career came in one of three forms: micro-assaults, micro-insults, or micro-invalidations. If they came in the form of micro-assaults, which are most likely to be conscious and deliberate, they are almost always spewed out in "private" situations that permit the perpetrator anonymity because of lack of witnesses. Most people will only verbalize micro-assaults publicly when they lose control of themselves or feel safe to engage in a micro-assault. For example, being called a "split-ass dyke" would be a micro-assault. I had been called that since I entered the CAF in 1987. A micro-insult is a subtle snub. Frequently, the perpetrator does not even know they have done this. Their message conveys a hidden insulting message. When I became a Command CWO, when all my peers were told they were great leaders, I was told that it was nice to have an academic on the council! This would be an example of a micro-insult. Micro-invalidation is the last of the three forms of micro-aggressions. Micro-invalidations, like micro-insults, are always unconscious. They usually exclude and invalidate the thoughts and feelings of a diverse person. For example, when I shared with a male counterpart how my contributions to the Corps were always overlooked, I was told not to be so oversensitive and that we should not be in it for ourselves. I almost laughed in this person's face, considering how he was always trying to get credit for other people's work.

    I faced micro-aggressions in every form my entire career, and whatever form they came in, they hurt. But instead of addressing the aggression on the spot I would pretend to ignore it. Growing up I watched and learned how to ignore uncomfortable situations. It was just too emotionally exhausting to deal with every single slight, with every passive-aggressive behaviour, and yet I knew in my heart that if I did not correct it, it would continue. When you ignore a certain behaviour, that behaviour becomes the new norm. The consequences of holding on to the burden of whether to call out the inappropriate behaviour or comment did not seem so taxing at the beginning of my career, but my rucksack got heavier and heavier with each micro-insult, invalidation, and assault that I packed away in there. The truth of the matter was that I did not have to deploy to some foreign land to face the enemy. I was fighting a war everyday at home against my own brothers in arms. I did not belong, no matter how good I was at my job. I did not look like them, I did not speak like them, despite trying to, and I did not act like them. Therefore, I would never be one of them, and they made sure I knew that.

Being forbidden to compete for the CAFCWO position was an absolute betrayal, but the penultimate betrayal was the competition for the VCDS Gp CWO job — a position I feel I got screwed out of twice because the rules appeared to change to achieve a desired result each time the appointment became available. Undoubtedly, there will be those of you who think I am complaining just because I did not get any of those jobs, but make no mistake, this is me expressing my frustration with the process and a need to expose the nepotism that goes on behind closed doors. Even at the most basic level there cannot be fair competition when the outcome is predetermined.

Nevertheless, on all four occasions I smiled and carried on, pretending it didn't bother me when it almost crushed me, especially the rejection of the VCDS CWO position. I had coveted this position since I was a Private. I saw it as the honest broker for the military. Where the RCN main concerns are ships, the CA's main concern being tanks, and the RCAF wanting new planes, the VCDS is responsible for ensuring that the finite resources serve the institution and not just one environment. I felt that was the perfect position for me. I was not the only one who thought I would have been a shoe-in for this job, especially since I had a proven track record as one of the most sought-after mentors in the CAF. Based on the unwritten and informal rules established in 2019 for this position regarding being the "first amongst equals" and being the mentor that the other Command CWOs relied upon, I feel I was the right person, with the right qualifications, to go into this job at that time. However, someone had a private agenda, so the system could not work the way it was supposed to — with transparency and according to the pre-existing rules.

14
IF IT WAS SO BAD, WHY STAY 35 YEARS?

Don't waste your time in anger, regrets, worries, and grudges. Life is too short to be unhappy.
— Roy T. Bennett

IF BEING IN THE CAF WAS THAT BAD, why did I stay so long? This is a question I am sure some of you are asking, and I don't blame you. I would be asking the same thing if I wasn't the author. I came out of the womb knowing I wanted to join the military and be a military police officer. From a very young age and as a result of my upbringing, I was driven by justice. For thirty-five years I got to live that dream! I did not do this job for money. I did it for the honour of wearing our military's uniform with the Canadian flag blazoned on my shoulder. Despite everything that has happened to me or that I permitted others to do to me, I was still able to find happiness for much of my career. Finding that place didn't only provide contentment but made me more motivated and better equipped to do the best job possible.

    I thoroughly enjoyed the work I did, whether it was as a MP, leading people, or as the person responsible for coming up with ideas on how to improve CAF common leadership training and everything in between. I loved many of the people I worked with. Being a member of the profession of arms was not a job for me, it was a calling. I was inspired to grow and be better, and I was always proud of the work that I did for this institution, regardless of who got credit for it.

    Most importantly, I got to partake in some of the greatest experiences of my life. I was given an opportunity to be a young role model by instructing at the MP Academy, and I was provided with opportunities throughout my career to experience unfamiliar cultures and ways of life. I got to work with some tremendous people. I have empathized with people whose country was at war; I have helped soldiers, sailors, and aviators transition from a warzone so that they were ready to reintegrate with their families back home; I have held jobs that have enriched my knowledge and self. I have jumped out of an airplane and even landed aircraft on a simulator (not very successfully, mind you). I thought I understood stress, but it only took about ten seconds after I sat down in the Air Traffic Controller seat for my deodorant to wear off! I partook in the construction of a wooden aircraft wing with the aircraft structures technicians. I got to walk the red carpet. At my Change of Appointment ceremony at 16 Wing Borden, the members of that Wing arranged for a fifty-person Honour Guard for when I showed up at the RCAF Museum to do my change of appointment. I was inducted into the Order of Military Merit, given the opportunity to go back to school full-time, and I was chosen as the first woman to mentor on the NATO advanced senior leadership course, held in Lucerne, Switzerland. I was named one of the top twenty women in defence. I got to visit the Central Intelligence Agency, the Pentagon, the Defence Intelligence Agency, and the National Geospatial Agency. Most importantly, when I reached the rank of CWO, I was given the honour and privilege of wearing my mentor's (CWO Colleen Halpin's) ranks on my designated environmental uniform and my Mess Dress at the Divisional and Command levels. I have since passed them on to two of my mentees.

I am very fortunate to have lived my dream and done what I loved because most people don't get that opportunity. As I said earlier, I came out of the womb knowing I wanted to join the military. I have never been a civilian, as we say, because of my deep emotional connection to this work. Looking back now from my civilian driver's seat, I only have two regrets. One, that I allowed people to claim my work as there own. When I was serving, I used to tell myself that didn't matter, but if I am being honest with myself, it did bother me. It mattered because it was a question of integrity. For example, when the CAF champion for women, peace, and security gives a brief to the entire CPO1/CWO Corps on Inclusion and all the material used came from a paper I had written for the Canadian Military Journal a few years prior, it is annoying when there is no credit to the author. What is worse is that the CAFCWO and the VCDS CWO were gushing over the presentation to the General. When I confronted the CAFCWO, he stated, "Oh I thought is seemed familiar." I did learn, when I asked for a copy of the General's presentation, that my name was listed on the last slide as a reference; however, people who had seen the presentation multiple times told me the last slide is never shown. Unfortunately, this happened to me more often than not. The CAFCWO council claimed credit for my work on the "Preferred Path" when we presented it to the CDS Executive. As a senior CWO, I created approximately nine major projects, none of which I got credit for. The only thing I regret is that I allowed my last three years to seriously taint my experience. I became emotionally inaccessible and numb due to the treatment I received. Since most people would never have guessed that I suffered like I did, I obviously did a great job at internalizing the feeling of not being wanted or being good enough for my dream profession. I became an expert at compartmentalizing all that pain and suffering, to my own detriment. But I refused to walk away, even if it killed me.

15
Trusted to Serve

Courage is the most important of all the virtues because without courage, you can't practice any other virtue consistently.
— *Maya Angelou*

MILITARY SERVICE IS A PRIVILEGE. From the time I entered the Forces, I was taught to operate within a team, to trust others to create cohesion in the face of adversity. I embraced this privilege, but a teammate ruined that for me when they abused my trust. I tried very hard, even after being let down by many of my supposed teammates, to continue to act in accordance with a set of principles, values, and professional expectations. After some intense therapy I can now say with hand on heart that when I state I was a professional within the profession of arms, I know in my heart that I earned that title and I wore it with pride despite having been abused and assaulted for no other reason than I was different from the majority.

According to the CAF's newest document, Trusted to Serve, the CAF is finally fully committed to creating a workplace that is welcoming, inclusive, safe, and respectful — for every member of the Defence Team. It is believed that it will improve and increase the institution's operational effectiveness. This new CAF document uses seventeen elements categorized as three ethical principles, six military values, and eight professional expectations to explain how and why the CAF and it's members can be trusted to serve. The three ethical principles consist of respecting the dignity of all persons, serving Canada before self, and obeying and supporting lawful authority. These principles also form part of the Department of National

Defence Ethics Program. The six military values include loyalty, courage, integrity, inclusion, and accountability. Lastly, the eight professional expectations that are considered a military member's duty, to aid them in putting the mission first, consist of accepting unlimited liability, fighting spirit, leadership, discipline, teamwork, readiness, and stewardship.

I am encouraged by this new doctrine, produced by the Canadian Defence Academy. To me, it means that the CAF is finally accepting that its responsibility in ensuring everyone who is part of, or who wants to be part of, the CAF will be respected and treated no different than another member of the CAF. The best part of this document is that it is written in a language that the newest recruit to the oldest and most senior officer can understand and, more importantly, implement.

This was not always the case. When I joined the Canadian Armed Forces, I was instructed to read and sign dozens of forms before I swore my oath of allegiance and headed off to Cornwallis for my recruit training. One of those papers I was required to sign referred to this abstract construct called a military ethos. I suspect, like most young people from my generation, I just signed it and never gave this thing a second thought. That is until much later in my career. Because I did not understand its function within the Profession of Arms, I did not always subscribe to these attributes. I did not always act in a professional manner, nor was I held to that, and I defaulted to protecting my buddies and myself. Obviously, others did the same thing, because throughout my career, I watched as others committed transgressions that did not comply to the CAF's ethos. So, change was inevitable.

Throughout my career my dignity was not respected nor were my differences welcomed. To be called a CUNT and to be told that I should have been exterminated with the Jews because I was a lesbian did not make me feel safe. Yet, despite everything that happened to me, I still served Canada before self. Once I learned to be a servant leader, I put others ahead of myself to ensure mission success. The ethical principle in Trusted to Serve of obeying and supporting lawful authority did not seem to resonate with the individual who believed it was their right to sexually assault me. He put himself before me, before the CAF, and before this country when he decided I had what he wanted and he was going to take it regardless of what the law said. Worst of all was that I was taught to protect him. I was taught that this was loyalty to the team.

The military value of loyalty was often confused with protecting your friends, your unit, your occupation, etc., instead of challenging unacceptable behaviour when you saw it. For example, when that WO told the joke about the difference between a lesbian and a lawyer while on our leadership course, everyone laughed, including myself — not because the joke was that funny but because I felt very alone. If you were different, you did not deserve loyalty from those who made up the majority, but you were expected to give it. When the CAFCWO chose to exclude me and highlight the contributions of the VCDS Gp CWO to the Corps in his comments to the future leaders of the CAF while at the Chief Warrant Officer Robert Osside Profession of Arms Institute, I remained the loyal soldier and never called him out to avoid embarrassing him in front of the class. Then again, I didn't have to react because CWOs Grant and Smith were having nothing of this exclusionary behaviour. They immediately stood up and spoke of my imminent retirement and my contributions to the NCM Corps.

People who are courageous speak out and correct things when something is wrong. I was not always courageous, and that is something I will have to live with. Just like CWOs Grant and Smith, when I saw some things that were so egregious, I had to speak up, regardless of the personal cost to me, such as telling the CAFCWO he had one opportunity to correct a decision that was driven by someone with a personal agenda that resulted in almost placing an anglophone into a truly francophone position. There was also the time that I called him out at a minister's round table when he told the CAF CWO Corps that I was the one who kept the rest of them in line when we spoke of culture. He took no responsibility for doing this.

Those who embody integrity take responsibility for their decisions and actions and accept the consequences, good or bad. There are numerous examples of others stealing my work during my time in the CAF, but here are a few examples: when the General Officer decided to present my work on inclusivity as their own and not give me credit for it; when a former leader of the CWO Corps decided that it was his idea to come up with the concept of the Preferred Path and the creation of the Corps CWO; when the CAFCWO took complete responsibility for the CAFCWO placement; and when a young MCpl boasted to me about how he investigated the break and enter of my neighbour in Borden when it had been my investigation. Why did they need to steal my work, when I would have given it to them if they had just credited my efforts?

Exclusivity breeds exclusion, while inclusion fosters belonging and connection. The Purge excluded me for being a lesbian, and then many CAF members who were considered my peers excluded me for being a woman. Naturally, there are those who are inclusive. When I was chosen to be the first female Cpl to be posted to the MP Academy, I met Cpl Marc Picard, who was the first male Cpl chosen. Marc was responsible for being the chief instructor for the English basic MP course, while I was responsible for the French course. Marc and I worked very well together. There was a mutual respect, and he was not threatened by me. He was very secure in his abilities, and we became very good friends. At the CWO level, I also had allies who made me feel included. These men, in my opinion, were and are some of the best CWOs the CAF has ever produced: CWO Kevin West, CPO Geoff McTigue, CWO Denis Gaudreault, CWO Gary Grant, CWO Jim Smith, CPO1 Tom Lizzote, CWO Kevin Mathers, CWO John Hall and CWO Johnny Ellis. I could go on and on but I think you get the picture. Some of these guys were ahead of their time while others are leading the way today. All of them were sincere, trustworthy, and honest, and acted on what they believed to be right. In my opinion and because of my dealings with them, I found them to be dedicated to fairness and justice, never using their official role for personal gain, and instead of making excuses, they made things right.

With young dedicated leaders such as some of the names listed above, the CAF is in good shape for the future. The other thing that is encouraging for the inclusion of diverse groups is the recent creation on the Chief of Personnel Conduct and Culture (CPCC) Command, along with the publication of Trusted to Serve. CPCC will hold those who cannot commit to the elements of the CAF ethos to account. Good or bad, CAF personnel have an obligation to be reliable and, most especially, accountable. The CAF needs all it's members to live by the ethos and to help others who are struggling to understand or to adopt the CAF ethos. This can and should be done by routinely having discussions about it's application. It is too late for me, but maybe it isn't too late for that young girl dreaming of one day wearing the uniform of the Canadian Armed Forces.

As I undergo treatment for my anxiety, depression, PTSD, c-PTSD and my sadness thinking I failed in my duty to the people of the CAF, to be an agent for change, I am learning that I actually did not fail in my duty. Hand on heart I can say that I put the mission first, including it's people. I hope I live long enough to see the day when all senior leaders of the CAF can say the same thing.

16
MY FINAL FAREWELL

Owning our story and loving ourselves through that process is the bravest thing we'll ever do.
— *Brené Brown*

I AM GRATEFUL FOR MY MILITARY SERVICE. It made me who I am today: a spouse, a stepmother, a grandmother, a daughter, a sister, a leader, a mentor, an author, and a proud veteran. I am also thankful that the individual who hissed at me that I should have been "exterminated with the Jews" was not able to carry out his despicable threat. For much of my career, I hated myself, and it culminated in the last three years of my career. I was too vulnerable to share my authentic self because I could not control the outcome. I was on the brink of attempting suicide. Today, I own my story.

On June 15, 2022, after almost thirty-five years of serving Queen and Country, and with most of the burdens removed from my rucksack, I proudly and happily said goodbye to the Canadian Forces, to the only life I had known. I did not actually think I would make it to that day, but I'm thankful that I did.

I wanted the day to be a day to remember and I believe I achieved that. I went out the same way I came in: being hopeful that this beloved organization would change for the better. My speech had people in the audience laughing and crying and listening with anticipation of what I would say next. That is, except for one of the most senior NCM in the CAF, who was caught on camera sleeping on and off throughout the ceremony.

There were seventy-five people at my Change of Appointment ceremony. In my speech I wanted people to know what my path was like, but more importantly, that we have great people in this institution. I thanked those who played a significant role in my career development and success, and I also explained just how much this great institution has changed since I was being hunted for being a homosexual. I went on to explain that when I first joined the CAF all I wanted to be was a MP. However, as time went on and I met and received mentorship from some amazing individuals, I soon realized I wanted to be more than a police officer, I wanted to be a leader in the CAF. I wanted to finish my career as a Level 1 Command CWO, and I accomplished that — albeit at a cost. The constant struggle to have a voice, to be seen, and to be heard took its toll. It almost cost me my life. In fact, the last match in the powder barrel was when I was completely ignored by the two most senior CPO1/CWO on the inner council after I learned that I did not get the VCDS CWO job. The job that, according to both of them, I was perfect for.

My final comments revolved around diversity, equity, and inclusion. I told the audience that when I looked back over the past thirty-five years, I could say we had come so far. I asked them to just think about the irony of me standing in front of them. Way back in 1987, I joined the very trade that was hunting gay people, and now in 2022, I was retiring as the Command CWO from the very command that would have been responsible for taking my security clearance away if the MPs ever found me hiding in plain sight. Moreover, I went on to point out the great evolution in diversity by asking all the female NCMs in the audience to stand, and when they did, I quietly explained that these were but a few CAF leaders who persevered and overcame adversity and obstacles for the privilege of serving.

My final statement to this audience was that I just wanted to be effective and to have influence. I wanted all women to not have to go through what I did. I finished my service in the CAF by imploring the leadership to ensure that if we ask women to stand on guard for Canada, they, as part of the CAF, must stand on guard for our servicewomen. The guests responded with a five-minute standing ovation.

After the signing of the change of appointment certificate, I relinquished my duties as the Command CWO and was officially out of a job in the CAF. We proceeded to my Retirement Departure with Dignity (DWD) ceremony. These ceremonies were launched by the Chief of the Defence Staff in 2003 "to formalize the [retirement] process and to ensure that CAF members are given the appropriate recognition upon completion of their military service."[2] Every service member who has completed basic recruit training and is being honourably released qualifies for a DWD.

At my DWD, people said wonderful things about me, but to be fair, anyone who opts for a DWD gets wonderful things said about them. Both our daughters got up and spoke about their experiences as children in a military family and both stated that I was their hero. I cried. Having listened to the master of ceremonies read a few letters that were written to me and then having read all the other ones that were sent in, I noticed a pattern. Every person spoke of my leadership, compassion, and mentorship. Despite certain individuals trying hard to convince me that I did not belong in their military, I did belong! Despite certain people stealing my work and claiming it as their own, those who really mattered knew the reality. The reality was that the only people who saw me as a fraud was myself and those who tried to exterminate me. The individuals who attended my DWD and those who have reached out to me since I retired have convinced me that all the self-loathing and guilt was for not.

It was ironic that on the day I retired from the CAF I was feeling the most welcomed. I was getting a glimpse of myself as others saw me. During the presentation portion of the DWD, I was so fortunate to be named an Honorary Intelligence Operator by the Strategic Advisor and the Branch CWO of the Intelligence Branch. This, I am told, is a rare occurrence, and since its inception they have only named twenty individuals as either Honorary Intelligence Officers or Honorary Intelligence Operators. I am HO20! James Bond has nothing on me! I also received a handmade quilt titled "Strong

---

[2] Mishall Rehman, "Changes to Depart With Dignity Program," *Canadian Military Family Magazine*, cmfmag.ca/policy/changes-to-depart-with-dignity-program/.

and Free." The quilt has my name sewn into it, along with words that the quilter, CWO Shelley Lamothe, said reminded her of me: loyal, professional, mentor, leader, friend, kind, partner, integrity, courage, strength, and compassionate. Two of my dear friends and mentees, CWO Johnny Ellis and CWO Sandra Bouchard, melted down some of their own gold and made me a set of gold dog tags, which they knew I wanted. I had a pair but unfortunately lost them. I also received two watches, a pocket watch from the Warrant Officer and Sergeant's Mess that had the very simple yet very meaningful inscription "she served her country" engraved on its face, while the other was a Treehut watch that the CFINTCOM Unit CWOs purchased and had the Latin word oraculi engraved on the back.

The Military Police Branch presented me with my badge that was originally issued to me on February 6, 1989. When I assumed my SJS position in 2014, I had to return my badge to the CFPM as I was no longer considered a MP. I was reclassified to a senior appointed CWO. The badge was in rough shape, but it is now back with me where it belongs. The CFPM presented me with a handpainted Thunderbird Mask by Richard Shorty, a well-known and sought-after Northern Tutchone First Nations artist. The members of the Intelligence Command flew the Intelligence Branch flag in my honour at all the bases that fall under CFINTCOM and at 16 Wing Borden, where CWO Geoff Rusconi was the Wing CWO. Geoff was a meteorological technician, a trade that falls inside the Intelligence Branch.

For my Change of Appointment ceremony, 16 Wing also surprised me by making me a drill cane. The cane, made by Sgt Jacob Abusow, was constructed using the wood from the Royal Flying Corps hangars, built in 1917. These hangars, which were an essential element of the first Canadian military aerodrome, were erected as temporary facilities at Camp Borden, the birthplace of the RCAF, and housed various air training schools.

I donated the drill cane to the Command CWO office of CFINTCOM for future Change of Appointment ceremonies, leaving a little piece of myself and my beloved 16 Wing Borden at CFINTCOM. I received champagne and some gift cards to a fancy restaurant in downtown Ottawa, which Judi used before leaving Ottawa for our final move to Kelowna, BC.

I was also given a customized, handcrafted knife set, along with a personalized charcuterie board with my name on it. Of all the tokens of appreciation, the most meaningful to me were the letters that people wrote to acknowledge my service. Most of the messages reflected on how my leadership touched people's lives and that my compassion and my drive to build leaders, not followers, inspired others to lead in the same manner. Finally, that my willingness to mentor people gave them a better sense of connection. While still serving, I would have read those letters and thought they were all lies. Today, I am learning to accept the praise at face value. I am learning to accept the moniker of "Trailblazer."

Epilogue

Healing may not be so much about getting better, as about letting go of everything that isn't you — all of the expectations, all of the beliefs — and becoming who you are.
— *Rachel Naomi Remen*

DURING MY LIFE, and especially during my career, I let certain people control me; I gave "them" permission to ignore me. Why you might ask? One of my favourite authors, Brené Brown, summed it up best when she said, "Shame derives its power from being unspeakable." I was made to feel ashamed of myself when I was young, and as such, I allowed my shame of being a lesbian to define me. Those who wanted nothing more than to expel me from their midst used this toxic shame that festered inside me to their benefit, because the last thing I wanted to do was bring it into the open. I was afraid, and they could smell blood in the water. Despite this, with the help of my therapist, we tackled that uncomfortable sensation in the pit of my stomach, because navigating all of shame's complexities was like trying on a thousand different versions of myself, with none feeling exactly right.

There is one version of me that no longer fit, which was when I was presented with my quilt of valour. My mind rushed right back to the stolen valour incident, and although I never said anything to the presenter, I confessed to my spouse afterward what I had done. When the presenter draped that quilt around me all I could think to do was smile and pretend, like I have always done. But deep down I knew that I did not deserve this honour. A quilt of valour is a hug from a grateful nation and a tribute to an injured Canadian Armed Forces member, past or present. I have yet to wrap myself in that quilt since the presenter draped it over my shoulders. In fact, I have not even touched it and I will not until I can wholly forgive myself for my past transgression of committing the act of stolen valour when I got on that service flight with Tracy and wore a Canadian Armed Forces uniform, pretending to be a member of the Profession of Arms. I still have a long road ahead of me but I have taken those first very difficult steps down that path.

My therapist helped me to realize that the reason I stayed and endured the exclusionary and toxic treatment was because I wanted to be an agent of change. I wanted to help lead the institution by inspiring and influencing others. I realized that I could touch more people through writing than I ever could in person. My pen could not be silenced like my mouth was every time I did not agree with the majority. Shortly after my release date on August 31, 2022, my wife and I loaded up the SUV and headed to our new home in the Okanagan. We purchased a home in West Kelowna that had an already established Airbnb. At my behest, Judi retired to look after me and run Sundance Sweet, her Airbnb. I enrolled in the local college, where I took social media training to help her with the advertising of her new business.

I have cut way down on my drinking, and for the most part do not have the urge to get drunk anymore. I go to therapy to help me learn to forgive myself. Most importantly, I am starting to recognize that acknowledging my shame is the first step in my recovery process. Thanks to BGen Simon Trudeau, when he invited me home to the MP Branch to speak with his senior leaders about leadership, I was given the platform to speak my shame aloud for the first time ever. Having done it once made the subsequent times easier and easier. The next step is believing that I did my utmost to live by the CAF ethos, every day and in everything I did, whether in or out of uniform. One incredibly special person told me that "the biggest payment a good leader can hope to receive is the respect of one's superiors, peers, and subordinates." Thanks to my Depart with Dignity, and the requests for advice I still receive in retirement, I now know I have that.

I still have a long road to travel to get back to health, both physically and mentally, but if I want to recover, I must accept shame and its irrationality in my life. I have started to do that. On the day I retired, my leadership work culminated in a few job offers. All my life's work was being rewarded with an invitation to write leadership doctrine, and my ability to create leaders instead of followers was being acknowledged by the Military Police Branch with an invitation to mentor Developmental Period 1, MP Course 2301. The course is named the "Belanger Platoon." Judi and I are getting along better than ever. I volunteer at our local Legion, and most importantly, I am starting to see life through sober eyes for the first time in a long, long time.

Without vodka running through my blood stream constantly, I recognized that I needed to share my story. Many people are suffering in silence. I have learned that we don't need to be silent — we have nothing to be ashamed of. We did nothing wrong! With that little nugget and having retired my "suit of armour" for good, it seems that each day that passes, my rucksack gets lighter and lighter. For those of you still struggling to lighten the load of your own rucksacks, I hope my story inspires you to one day tell your story. I would also like for others to continue to inspire change. I want others to understand the influence that their actions have on others. If you recognize yourself in this story, I ask that you learn from this and endeavour to not repeat these toxic behaviours in the future.

SECURITAS!

Acknowledgements

A SOLDIER NEVER FIGHTS A WAR ALONE, and while I may have started this battle by myself, I certainly would not have gained ground on the enemy without the support of a few people, namely: my family; Maj (Ret'd) Colleen Halpin for always picking up the telephone when I called for advice; BGen Simon Trudeau for giving me a platform to speak my shame in public for the very first time; my primary care physician, Dr. Carolyn Brownlee, for being so caring, professional, and most importantly, thorough; and my psychologist, Dr. Lynette Monteiro, who, through her sage advice, guided me in exercises so I could help myself and just listened, without ever judging me, as I gave my shame a voice.

To every person who grew up wanting to serve their country but was told they could not because they suffered from the disease of homosexuality, a condition deviating from "normal" heterosexual behaviour, this book is dedicated to you; to Michelle Douglas for having the courage to take on the government when she was told she could no longer serve; and to Martine Roy, who believed that she could demand an apology from the Government of Canada and get it. It is because of women like you two that I was able to serve a full career. I stood on your shoulders, and for that I offer you my utmost thanks.

Thank you as well to those who chose to ignore the bigotry, but who had to hide in plain sight, avoiding the Special Investigation

Unit (SIU) and the Royal Canadian Mounted Police (RCMP) throughout the LGBT Purge that put such a black mark on this country's reputation. It is also for all those women out there who just want an opportunity to be treated as equals.

This book would not have come together without the steadfast help of LCol (Ret'd) Bill Cummings. Bill, in the words of Brené Brown, thank you for convincing me that "people who wade into discomfort and vulnerability and tell the truth about their stories are the real badasses." In my own words, thank you for being the expert on our military ethos and making sure I was honest with myself and that I gave my shame a name. Thank you for being a good friend.

To my family: Dad, in a perverse way, thank you for preparing me to excel in the Canadian Armed Forces. To my sister and brother, words cannot express how much I love you both, and I especially want to thank you for allowing me to tell this story, but more importantly, for taking the brunt of the abuse so I didn't have to. To my mother, I know you have stood beside me every day before and since May 23, 2012, because I have felt your presence. Most especially, when I thought I could not take another step, I felt you lift me up and carry me. I miss you.

Most importantly, this book is dedicated to my beautiful wife Judi and our children, whose constant love and support kept me from tumbling into the abyss. Judi, you are my soulmate and I love you. None of this would have been possible without you, nor would I have ever made it as long or as far as I did without your loving support and patience, especially of late. There is no one I would have rather taken this ride with. Jessica and Kayla, thank you both for forgiving my transgressions from your childhood and for loving me despite never being there for either of you. You are amazing young women, and I am so very proud of both of you.

Additional Reading

IF YOU WOULD LIKE TO READ my other published written works, they can be found in the following leadership journals:

Belanger, Necole. "The Accidental Strategic Chief Petty Officer/Chief Warrant Officer." *Canadian Military Journal* 16, no. 3 (2016): 66–71. journal.forces.gc.ca/vol16/no3/PDF/CMJ163Ep66.pdf.

———. "Being a Member of the Profession of Arms. A RCAF Chief Warrant Officer's Perspective." Royal Military College Saint-Jean. Updated October 20, 2022. cmrsj-rmcsj.forces.gc.ca/cb-bk/art-art/2016/art-art-2016-9-eng.asp.

———. "Deciphering the Roles of Chief Petty Officers/Chief Warrant Officers within Command Teams." *Canadian Military Journal* 21, no. 4 (2021): 41–50. journal.forces.gc.ca/PDFs/CMJ214Ep41.pdf.

———. "Inclusive Leadership": If We Build It Will They Come?" *Canadian Military Journal* 19, no. 1 (2018): 32–39. journal.forces.gc.ca/vol19/no1/eng/PDF/CMJ191Ep32.pdf.

About the Author

NECOLE BELANGER is a retired Command Chief Warrant Officer of the Canadian Armed Forces (CAF), who joined at the tail end of the LGBTQ Purge, which saw more than 9000 members of the RCMP, CAF, and Federal Public Service employees have their lives and careers destroyed because of a government-sanctioned practice to label them as threats to national security. CCWO (Ret'd) Belanger managed to hide in plain sight and completed 35 years of service to her country.

She is a graduate of the Law and Security Administration program from Loyalist College of Applied Arts and Technology in Belleville, ON. She has a Bachelor of Military Arts and Science degree from the Royal Military College, Kingston, ON, and is a graduate of the non-commissioned member (NCM) executive professional development program, the executive leadership program, the Canadian security studies program, and the complete leadership program series from the CWO Robert Profession of Arms Institute. She has published leadership articles for the Canadian Military Journal and the Royal Canadian Air Force Journal and is the single most published NCM author in the CAF.

She currently resides in Kelowna, BC with her wife of 29 years, where they run a licensed AirBnB together when not visiting with their two precious granddaughters and daughters.

DOUBLE‡DAGGER
— www.doubledagger.ca —

DOUBLE DAGGER BOOKS is Canada's only military-focused publisher. Conflict and warfare have shaped human history since before we began to record it. The earliest stories that we know of, passed on as oral tradition, speak of war, and more importantly, the essential elements of the human condition that are revealed under its pressure.

We are dedicated to publishing material that, while rooted in conflict, transcend the idea of "war" as merely a genre. Fiction, non-fiction, and stuff that defies categorization, we want to read it all.

Because if you want peace, study war.

Manufactured by Amazon.ca
Bolton, ON

36169972R00090